# The OUTSIDERS

# The OUTSIDERS

Eight
Unconventional CEOs
and Their
Radically Rational
Blueprint for Success

William N. Thorndike, Jr.

HARVARD BUSINESS REVIEW PRESS

BOSTON, MASSACHUSETTS

Library of Congress Cataloging-in-Publication Data

Thorndike, William.
    The outsiders : eight unconventional CEOs and their radically rational blueprint for success / William N. Thorndike, Jr.
        p. cm.
    ISBN 978-1-4221-6267-5 (alk. paper)
    1. Executive ability.   2. Industrial management.   3. Success in business.
4. Chief executive officers—Biography.   I. Title.
    HD38.2.T476 2012
    658.4'09—dc23

                                                            2012012451

# Contents

# Preface: Singletonville

It's almost impossible to overpay the truly extraordinary CEO . . . but the species is rare.

—*Warren Buffett*

You are what your record says you are.

—*Bill Parcells*

Success leaves traces.

—*John Templeton*

Who's the greatest CEO of the last fifty years?

If you're like most people, the overwhelming likelihood is that you answered, "Jack Welch," and it's easy to see why. Welch ran General Electric, one of America's most iconic companies, for twenty years, from 1981 to 2001. GE's shareholders prospered mightily during Welch's tenure, with a compound annual return of *20.9 percent*. If you had invested a dollar in GE stock when Welch became CEO, that dollar would have been worth an extraordinary *$48* when he turned the reins over to his successor, Jeff Immelt.

Welch was both an active manager and a master corporate ambassador. He was legendarily peripatetic, traveling constantly to visit GE's far-flung operations, tirelessly grading managers and shuffling them between business units, and developing companywide strategic initiatives with exotic-sounding names like "Six Sigma" and "TQM." Welch had a lively, pugnacious personality and enjoyed his interactions with Wall Street and the business press. He was very comfortable in the limelight, and during his tenure at GE, he frequently appeared on the cover of *Fortune* magazine. Since his retirement, he has remained in the headlines with occasional controversial pronouncements on a variety of business topics including the performance of his successor. He has also written two books of management advice with typically combative titles like *Straight from the Gut.*

With this combination of notoriety and excellent returns, Welch has become a de facto gold standard for CEO performance exemplifying a particular approach to management, one that emphasizes active oversight of operations, regular communication with Wall Street, and an intense focus on stock price. Is he, however, the greatest chief executive of the last fifty years?

The answer is an emphatic no.

To understand why, it's important to start by offering up a new, more precise way to measure CEO ability. CEOs, like professional athletes, compete in a highly quantitative field, and yet there is no single, accepted metric for measuring their performance, no equivalent of ERA for baseball pitchers, or complication rate for surgeons, or goals against average for hockey goalies.

The business press doesn't attempt to identify the top performers in any rigorous way.

Instead, they generally focus on the largest, best-known companies, the *Fortune* 100, which is why the executives of those companies are so often found on the covers of the top business magazines. The metric that the press usually focuses on is growth in revenues and profits. It's the increase in a company's *per share value,* however, not growth in sales or earnings or employees, that offers the ultimate barometer of a CEO's greatness. It's as if *Sports Illustrated* put only the tallest pitchers and widest goalies on its cover.

In assessing performance, what matters isn't the absolute rate of return but the return relative to peers and the market. You really only need to know three things to evaluate a CEO's greatness: the compound annual return to shareholders during his or her tenure and the return over the same period for peer companies and for the broader market (usually measured by the S&P 500).

Context matters greatly—beginning and ending points can have an enormous impact, and Welch's tenure coincided almost exactly with the epic bull market that began in late 1982 and continued largely uninterrupted until early 2000. During this remarkable period, the S&P averaged a 14 percent annual return, roughly double its long-term average. It's one thing to deliver a 20 percent return over a period like that and quite another to deliver it during a period that includes several severe bear markets.

A baseball analogy helps to make this point. In the steroid-saturated era of the mid- to late 1990s, twenty-nine home runs was a pretty mediocre level of offensive output (the leaders consistently hit over sixty). When Babe Ruth did it in 1919, however, he shattered the prior record (set in 1884) and changed baseball forever, ushering in the modern power-oriented game. Again, context matters.

The other important element in evaluating a CEO's track record is performance relative to peers, and the best way to assess this is by comparing a CEO with a broad universe of peers. As in the game of duplicate bridge, companies competing within an industry are usually dealt similar hands, and the long-term differences between them, therefore, are more a factor of managerial ability than external forces.

Let's look at an example from the mining industry. It's almost impossible to compare the performance of a gold mining company CEO in 2011, when gold prices topped out at over $1,900 an ounce, with that of an executive operating in 2000, when prices languished at $400. CEOs in the gold industry cannot control the price of the underlying commodity. They must simply do the best job for shareholders, given the hand the market deals them, and in assessing performance, it's most useful to compare CEOs with other executives operating under the same conditions.

When a CEO generates significantly better returns than both his peers and the market, he deserves to be called "great," and by this definition, Welch, who outperformed the S&P by 3.3 times over his tenure at GE, was an undeniably great CEO.

He wasn't even in the same zip code as Henry Singleton, however.

. . .

Known today only to a small group of investors and cognoscenti, Henry Singleton was a remarkable man with an unusual background for a CEO. A world-class mathematician who enjoyed playing chess blindfolded, he had programmed MIT's first computer while earning a doctorate in electrical engineering. During World War II, he developed a "degaussing" technology that allowed Allied ships to avoid radar detection, and in the 1950s, he created an inertial guidance system that is still in use in most military and commercial aircraft. All that before he founded a conglomerate, Teledyne, in the early 1960s and became one of history's great CEOs.

Conglomerates were the Internet stocks of the 1960s, when large numbers of them went public. Singleton, however, ran a very unusual conglomerate. Long before it became popular, he aggressively repurchased his stock, eventually buying in over *90 percent* of Teledyne's shares; he avoided dividends, emphasized cash flow over reported earnings, ran a famously decentralized organization, and never split the company's stock, which for much of the 1970s and 1980s was the highest priced on the New York Stock Exchange (NYSE). He was known as "the Sphinx" for his reluctance to speak with either analysts or journalists, and he never once appeared on the cover of *Fortune* magazine.

Singleton was an iconoclast, and the idiosyncratic path he chose to follow caused much comment and consternation on Wall Street and in the business press. It turned out that he was right to ignore the skeptics. The long-term returns of his better-known peers were generally mediocre—averaging only 11 percent per annum, a small improvement over the S&P 500.

Singleton, in contrast, ran Teledyne for almost thirty years, and the annual compound return to his investors was an extraordinary *20.4 percent*. If you had invested a dollar with Singleton in 1963, by 1990, when he retired as chairman in the teeth of a severe bear market, it would have been worth *$180*. That same dollar invested in a broad group of conglomerates would have been worth only $27, and $15 if invested in the S&P 500. Remarkably, Singleton outperformed the index by *over twelve times*.

Using our definition of success, Singleton was a greater CEO than Jack Welch. His numbers are simply better: not only were his per share returns higher relative to the market and his peers, but he sustained them over a longer period of time (twenty-eight years versus Welch's twenty) and in a market environment that featured several protracted bear markets.

His success did not stem from Teledyne's owning any unique, rapidly growing businesses. Rather, much of what distinguished Singleton from his peers lay in his mastery of the critical but somewhat mysterious field of *capital allocation*—the process of deciding how to deploy the firm's resources to earn the best possible return for shareholders. So let's spend a minute explaining what capital allocation is and why it's so important and why so few CEOs are really good at it.

· · ·

CEOs need to do two things well to be successful: run their operations efficiently and deploy the cash generated by those operations. Most CEOs (and the management books they write or read) focus on managing operations, which is undeniably important. Singleton, in contrast, gave most of his attention to the latter task.

Basically, CEOs have five essential choices for deploying capital—investing in existing operations, acquiring other businesses, issuing dividends, paying down debt, or repurchasing stock—and three alternatives for raising it—tapping internal cash flow, issuing debt, or raising equity. Think of these options collectively as a tool kit. Over the long term, returns for shareholders will be determined largely by the decisions a CEO makes in choosing which tools to use (and which to avoid) among these various options. Stated simply, two companies with identical operating results and different approaches to allocating capital will derive two very different long-term outcomes for shareholders.

Essentially, capital allocation is investment, and as a result all CEOs are both capital allocators and investors. In fact, this role just might be the most important responsibility any CEO has, and yet despite its importance, *there are no courses on capital allocation at the top business schools.* As Warren Buffett has observed, very few CEOs come prepared for this critical task:

> *The heads of many companies are not skilled in capital allocation. Their inadequacy is not surprising. Most bosses rise to the top because they have excelled in an area such as marketing, production, engineering, administration, or sometimes, institutional politics. Once they become CEOs, they now must make capital allocation decisions, a critical job that they may have never tackled and that is not easily mastered. To stretch the point, it's as if the final step for a highly talented musician was not to perform at Carnegie Hall, but instead, to be named Chairman of the Federal Reserve.*[1]

This inexperience has a direct and significant impact on investor returns. Buffett stressed the potential impact of this skill gap, pointing out that "after ten years on the job, a CEO whose company annually retains earnings equal to 10 percent of net worth will have been responsible for the deployment of more than 60 percent of all the capital at work in the business."[2]

Singleton was a master capital allocator, and his decisions in navigating among these various allocation alternatives differed significantly from the decisions his peers were making and had an enormous positive impact on long-term returns for his shareholders. Specifically, Singleton focused Teledyne's capital on selective acquisitions and a series of large share repurchases. He was restrained in issuing shares, made frequent use of debt, and did not pay a dividend until the late 1980s. In contrast, the other conglomerates pursued a mirror-image allocation strategy—actively issuing shares to buy companies, paying dividends, avoiding share repurchases, and generally using less debt. In short, they deployed a different set of tools with very different results.

If you think of capital allocation more broadly as resource allocation and include the deployment of human resources, you find again that Singleton had a highly differentiated approach. Specifically, he believed in an extreme form of organizational decentralization with a wafer-thin corporate staff at headquarters and operational responsibility and authority concentrated in the general managers of the business units. This was very different from the approach of his peers, who typically had elaborate headquarters staffs replete with vice presidents and MBAs.

It turns out that the most extraordinary CEOs of the last fifty years, the truly great ones, shared this mastery of resource allocation. In fact, their approach was uncannily similar to Singleton's.

. . .

In 1988, Warren Buffett wrote an article on investors who shared a combination of excellent track records and devotion to the value investing principles of legendary Columbia Business School professors Benjamin Graham and David Dodd. Graham and Dodd's unorthodox investing strategy advocated buying companies that traded at material discounts to conservative assessments of their net asset values.

To illustrate the strong correlation between extraordinary investment returns and Graham and Dodd's principles, Buffett used the analogy of a national coin-flipping contest in which 225 million Americans, once a day, wager a dollar on a coin toss. Each day the losers drop out, and the next day the stakes grow as all prior winnings are bet on the next day's flips. After twenty days, there are 215 people left, each of whom has won a little over $1 million. Buffett points out that this outcome is purely the result of chance and that 225 million orangutans would have produced the same result. He then introduces an interesting wrinkle:

> *If you found, however, that 40 of them came from a particular zoo in Omaha, you would be pretty sure you were on to something. . . . Scientific inquiry naturally follows such a pattern. If you were trying to analyze possible causes of a rare type of cancer and you found that 400 cases occurred in some little mining town in Montana, you would get very interested in the water there, or the occupation of those afflicted, or other variables. I think you will find that a disproportionate number of successful coin-flippers in the investment world came from a very small intellectual village that could be called Graham-and-Doddsville.*[3]

If, as historian Laurel Ulrich has written, well-behaved women rarely make history, perhaps it follows that conventional CEOs rarely trounce the market or their peers. As in the world of investing, there are very few extraordinary managerial coin-flippers, and if you were to list them, not surprisingly, you would find they were also iconoclasts.

These managerial standouts, the ones profiled in this book, ran companies in both growing and declining markets, in industries as diverse as manufacturing, media, defense, consumer products, and financial services. Their companies ranged widely in terms of size and maturity. None had hot, easily repeatable retail concepts or intellectual property advantages versus their peers, and yet they hugely outperformed them.

Like Singleton, they developed unique, markedly different approaches to their businesses, typically drawing much comment and questioning from peers and the business press. Even more interestingly, although they developed these principles independently, it turned out they were iconoclastic in *virtually identical ways*. In other words, there seemed to be a pattern to their iconoclasm, a potential blueprint for success, one that correlated highly with extraordinary returns.

They seemed to operate in a parallel universe, one defined by devotion to a shared set of principles, a *worldview,* which gave them citizenship in a tiny intellectual village. Call it Singleton-ville, a very select group of men and women who understood, among other things, that:

- Capital allocation is a CEO's most important job.

- What counts in the long run is the increase in *per share value,* not overall growth or size.

- Cash flow, not reported earnings, is what determines long-term value.

- Decentralized organizations release entrepreneurial energy and keep both costs and "rancor" down.

- Independent thinking is essential to long-term success, and interactions with outside advisers (Wall Street, the press, etc.) can be distracting and time-consuming.

- Sometimes the best investment opportunity is your own stock.

- With acquisitions, patience is a virtue . . . as is occasional boldness.

Interestingly, their iconoclasm was reinforced in many cases by geography. For the most part, their operations were located in cities like Denver, Omaha, Los Angeles, Alexandria, Washington, and St. Louis, removed from the financial epicenter of the Boston/New York corridor. This distance helped insulate them from the din of Wall Street conventional wisdom. (The two CEOs who had offices in the Northeast shared this predilection for nondescript locations—Dick Smith's office was located in the rear of a suburban shopping mall; Tom Murphy's was in a former midtown Manhattan residence sixty blocks from Wall Street.)

The residents of Singletonville, our outsider CEOs, also shared an interesting set of personal characteristics: They were generally frugal (often legendarily so) and humble, analytical, and understated. They were devoted to their families, often leaving the office early to attend school events. They did not typically relish the outward-facing part of the CEO role. They did not give chamber of commerce speeches, and they did not attend Davos. They rarely appeared on the covers of business publications and did not write books of management advice. They were not cheerleaders or marketers or backslappers, and they did not exude charisma.

They were very different from high-profile CEOs such as Steve Jobs or Sam Walton or Herb Kelleher of Southwest Airlines or Mark Zuckerberg. These geniuses are the Isaac Newtons of business, struck apple-like by enormously powerful ideas that they proceed to execute with maniacal focus and determination. Their situations and circumstances, however, are not remotely similar (nor are the lessons from their careers remotely transferable) to those of the vast majority of business executives.

The outsider CEOs had neither the charisma of Walton and Kelleher nor the marketing or technical genius of Jobs or Zuckerberg. In fact, their circumstances were a lot like those of the typical American business executive. Their returns, however, were anything but quotidian. As figures P-1 and P-2 show, on

**FIGURE P-1**

## Multiple of S&P 500 total return

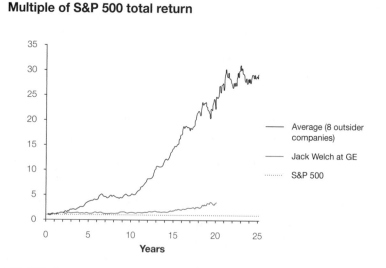

**FIGURE P-2**

## Multiple of peer group total return

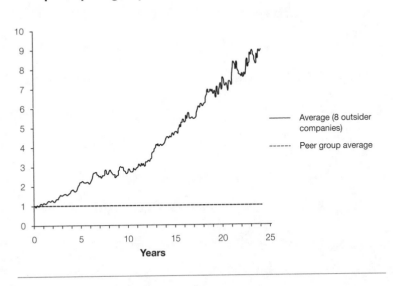

Average (8 outsider companies)

Peer group average

average they outperformed the S&P 500 by *over twenty times* and their peers by *over seven times*—and our focus will be on looking at how those returns were achieved. We will, as the Watergate informant Deep Throat suggested, "follow the money," looking carefully at the key decisions these outsider CEOs made to maximize returns to shareholders and the lessons those decisions hold for today's managers and entrepreneurs.

# Introduction

## *An Intelligent Iconoclasm*

It is impossible to produce superior performance
unless you do something *different*.

—*John Templeton*

*The New Yorker*'s Atul Gawande uses the term *positive deviant* to describe unusually effective performers in the field of medicine. To Gawande, it is natural that we should study these outliers in order to learn from them and improve performance.[1]

Surprisingly, in business the best are not studied as closely as in other fields like medicine, the law, politics, or sports. After studying Henry Singleton, I began, with the help of a talented group of Harvard MBA students, to look for other cases where one company handily beat both its peers and Jack Welch (in terms of relative market performance). It turned out, as Warren Buffett's quote in the preface suggests, that these companies (and CEOs) were rare as hen's teeth. After extensive searching in databases at Harvard Business School's Baker Library, we came across only seven other examples that passed these two tests.

Interestingly, like Teledyne, these companies were not generally well known. Nor were their CEOs despite the enormous gap between their performance and that of many of today's high-visibility chief executives.

. . .

The press portrays the successful, contemporary CEO, of which Welch is an exemplar, as a charismatic, action-oriented leader who works in a gleaming office building and is surrounded by an army of hardworking fellow MBAs. He travels by corporate jet and spends much of his time touring operations, meeting with Wall Street analysts, and attending conferences. The adjective *rock star* is often used to describe these fast-moving executives who are frequently recruited into their positions after well-publicized searches and usually come from top executive positions at well-known companies.

Since the collapse of Lehman Brothers in September 2008, this breed of high-profile chief executive has been understandably vilified. They are commonly viewed as being greedy (possibly fraudulent) and heartless as they fly around in corporate planes, laying off workers, and making large deals that often destroy value for stockholders. In short, they're seen as being a lot like Donald Trump on *The Apprentice*. On that reality television show, Trump makes no pretense about being avaricious, arrogant, and promotional. Not exactly a catalog of Franklinian values.

The residents of Singletonville, however, represent a refreshing rejoinder to this stereotype. All were first-time CEOs, most with very little prior management experience. Not one came to the job from a high-profile position, and all but one were new to their industries and companies. Only two had MBAs. As a group, they did not attract or seek the spotlight. Rather, they labored in relative obscurity and were generally appreciated by only a handful of sophisticated investors and aficionados.

As a group, they shared old-fashioned, premodern values including frugality, humility, independence, and an unusual combination of conservatism and boldness. They typically worked out of bare-bones offices (of which they were inordinately proud), generally eschewed perks such as corporate planes, avoided the spotlight wherever possible, and rarely communicated with Wall Street or the business press. They also actively avoided bankers and other advisers, preferring their own counsel and that of a select group around them. Ben Franklin would have liked these guys.

This group of happily married, middle-aged men (and one woman) led seemingly unexciting, balanced, quietly philanthropic lives, yet in their business lives they were neither conventional nor complacent. They were positive deviants, and they were deeply iconoclastic.

The word *iconoclast* is derived from Greek and means "smasher of icons." The word has evolved to have the more general meaning of someone who is determinedly different, proudly eccentric. The original iconoclasts came from outside the societies (and temples) where icons resided; they were challengers of societal norms and conventions, and they were much feared in ancient

Greece. The CEOs profiled in this book were not nearly so fearsome, but they did share interesting similarities with their ancient forbears: they were also outsiders, disdaining long-accepted conventional approaches (like paying dividends or avoiding share repurchases) and relishing their unorthodoxy.

Like Singleton, these CEOs consistently made very different decisions than their peers did. They were not, however, blindly contrarian. Theirs was an *intelligent iconoclasm* informed by careful analysis and often expressed in unusual financial metrics that were distinctly different from industry or Wall Street conventions.

In this way, their iconoclasm was similar to Billy Beane's as described by Michael Lewis in *Moneyball*.[2] Beane, the general manager of the perennially cash-strapped Oakland A's baseball team, used statistical analysis to gain an edge over his better-heeled competitors. His approach centered on new metrics—on-base and slugging percentages—that correlated more highly with team winning percentage than the traditional statistical troika of home runs, batting average, and runs batted in.

Beane's analytical insights influenced every aspect of how he ran the A's—from drafting and trading strategies to whether or not to steal bases or use sacrifice bunts in games (no, in both cases). His approach in all these areas was highly unorthodox, yet also highly successful, and his team, despite having the second-lowest payroll in the league, made the playoffs in four of his first six years on the job.

Like Beane, Singleton and these seven other executives developed unique, iconoclastic approaches to their businesses that drew much comment and questioning from peers and the business press. And, like Beane's, their results were exceptional, handily outperforming both the legendary Welch and their industry counterparts.

They came from a variety of backgrounds: one was an astronaut who had orbited the moon, one a widow with no prior business experience, one inherited the family business, two were highly quantitative PhDs, one an investor who'd never run a company before. They were all, however, new to the CEO role, and they shared a couple of important traits, including fresh eyes and a deep-seated commitment to rationality.

Isaiah Berlin, in a famous essay about Leo Tolstoy, introduced the instructive contrast between the "fox," who knows many things, and the "hedgehog," who knows one thing but knows it very well. Most CEOs are hedgehogs—they grow up in an industry and by the time they are tapped for the top role, have come to know it thoroughly. There are many positive attributes associated with hedgehogness, including expertise, specialization, and focus.

Foxes, however, also have many attractive qualities, including an ability to make connections across fields and to innovate, and the CEOs in this book were definite foxes. They had familiarity with other companies and industries and disciplines, and this ranginess translated into new perspectives, which in turn helped them to develop new approaches that eventually translated into exceptional results.

. . .

In the 1986 Berkshire Hathaway annual report, Warren Buffett looked back on his first twenty-five years as a CEO and concluded that the most important and surprising lesson from his career to date was the discovery of a mysterious force, the corporate equivalent of teenage peer pressure, that impelled CEOs to imitate the actions of their peers. He dubbed this powerful force the *institutional imperative* and noted that it was nearly ubiquitous, warning that effective CEOs needed to find some way to tune it out.

The CEOs in this book all managed to avoid the insidious influence of this powerful imperative. How? They found an antidote in a shared managerial philosophy, a *worldview* that pervaded their organizations and cultures and drove their operating and capital allocating decisions. Although they arrived at their management philosophies independently, what's striking is how remarkably similar the ingredients were across this group of executives despite widely varying industries and circumstances.

Each ran a highly decentralized organization; made at least one very large acquisition; developed unusual, cash flow–based metrics; and bought back a significant amount of stock. None paid meaningful dividends or provided Wall Street guidance. All received the same combination of derision, wonder, and skepticism from their peers and the business press. All also enjoyed eye-popping, credulity-straining performance over very long tenures (twenty-plus years on average).

The business world has traditionally divided itself into two basic camps: those who run companies and those who invest in them. The lessons of these iconoclastic CEOs suggest a new, more nuanced conception of the chief executive's job, with less emphasis placed on charismatic leadership and more on careful deployment of firm resources.

At bottom, these CEOs thought more like investors than managers. Fundamentally, they had confidence in their own analyti-

## A Distant Mirror: 1974–1982

In assessing the current relevance of these outsider CEOs, it's worth looking at how each navigated the post–World War II period that looks most like today's extended economic malaise: the brutal 1974–1982 period.

That period featured a toxic combination of an external oil shock, disastrous fiscal and monetary policy, and the worst domestic political scandal in the nation's history. This cocktail of negative news produced an eight-year period that saw crippling inflation, two deep recessions (and bear markets), 18 percent interest rates, a threefold increase in oil prices, and the first resignation of a sitting US president in over one hundred years. In the middle of this dark period, in August 1979, *BusinessWeek* famously ran a cover story titled "Are Equities Dead?"

The times, like now, were so uncertain and scary that most managers sat on their hands, but for all the outsider CEOs it was among the most active periods of their careers—*every single one* was engaged in either a significant share repurchase program or a series of large acquisitions (or in the case of Tom Murphy, both). As a group, they were, in the words of Warren Buffett, *very* "greedy" while their peers were deeply "fearful."[a]

a. Author interview with Warren Buffett, July 24, 2006.

cal skills, and on the rare occasions when they saw compelling discrepancies between value and price, they were prepared to act boldly. When their stock was cheap, they bought it (often in large quantities), and when it was expensive, they used it to buy other companies or to raise inexpensive capital to fund future growth.

If they couldn't identify compelling projects, they were comfortable waiting, sometimes for very long periods of time (an entire decade in the case of General Cinema's Dick Smith). Over the long term, this systematic, methodical blend of low buying and high selling produced exceptional returns for shareholders.

This reformulation of the CEO's job stemmed from shared (and unusual) backgrounds. All of these CEOs were outsiders. All were first-time chief executives (half not yet forty when they took the job), and all but one were new to their industries. They were not bound by prior experience or industry convention, and their collective records show the enormous power of fresh eyes. This freshness of perspective is an age-old catalyst for innovation across many fields. In science, Thomas Kuhn, inventor of the concept of the *paradigm shift,* found that the greatest discoveries were almost invariably made by newcomers and the very young (think of the middle-aged former printer, Ben Franklin, taming lightning; or Einstein, the twenty-seven-year-old patent clerk, deriving $E = mc^2$).

This fox-like outsider's perspective helped these executives develop differentiated approaches, and it informed their entire management philosophy. As a group, they were deeply independent, generally avoiding communication with Wall Street, disdaining the use of advisers, and preferring decentralized organizational structures that self-selected for other independent thinkers.

. . .

In his recent bestseller, *Outliers,* Malcolm Gladwell presents a rule of thumb that expertise across a wide variety of fields requires ten thousand hours of practice.[3] So how does the phenomenal success of this group of neophyte CEOs square with that heuristic? Certainly none of these CEOs had logged close to ten thousand hours as managers before assuming the top spot, and perhaps their success points to an important distinction between expertise and innovation.

Gladwell's rule is a guide to achieving mastery, which is not necessarily the same thing as innovation. As John Templeton's quote at the beginning of this chapter suggests, exceptional relative performance demands new thinking, and at the center of the worldview shared by these CEOs was a commitment to rationality, to analyzing the data, *to thinking for themselves*.

These eight CEOs were not charismatic visionaries, nor were they drawn to grandiose strategic pronouncements. They were practical and agnostic in temperament, and they systematically tuned out the noise of conventional wisdom by fostering a certain simplicity of focus, a certain *asperity* in their cultures and their communications. Scientists and mathematicians often speak of the clarity "on the other side" of complexity, and these CEOs—all of whom were quantitatively adept (more had engineering degrees than MBAs)—had a genius for simplicity, for cutting through the clutter of peer and press chatter to zero in on the core economic characteristics of their businesses.

In all cases, this led the outsider CEOs to focus on cash flow and to forgo the blind pursuit of the Wall Street holy grail of reported earnings. Most public company CEOs focus on maximizing quarterly reported net income, which is understandable since that is Wall Street's preferred metric. Net income, however, is a bit of a blunt instrument and can be significantly distorted by differences in debt levels, taxes, capital expenditures, and past acquisition history.

As a result, the outsiders (who often had complicated balance sheets, active acquisition programs, and high debt levels) believed the key to long-term value creation was to optimize free cash flow, and this emphasis on cash informed all aspects of how they ran their companies—from the way they paid for acquisitions and managed their balance sheets to their accounting policies and compensation systems.

This single-minded cash focus was the foundation of their iconoclasm, and it invariably led to a laser-like focus on a few select variables that shaped each firm's strategy, usually in entirely different directions from those of industry peers. For Henry Singleton in the 1970s and 1980s, it was stock buybacks; for John Malone, it was the relentless pursuit of cable subscribers; for Bill Anders, it was divesting noncore businesses; for Warren Buffett, it was the generation and deployment of insurance float.

At the core of their shared worldview was the belief that the primary goal for any CEO was to optimize long-term value *per share,* not organizational growth. This may seem like an obvious objective; however, in American business, there is a deeply ingrained urge to get *bigger.* Larger companies get more attention in the press; the executives of those companies tend to earn higher salaries and are more likely to be asked to join prestigious boards and clubs. As a result, it is very rare to see a company proactively shrink itself. And yet virtually all of these CEOs shrank their share bases significantly through repurchases. Most also shrank their operations through asset sales or spin-offs, and they were not shy about selling (or closing) underperforming divisions. Growth, it turns out, often doesn't correlate with maximizing shareholder value.

This pragmatic focus on cash and an accompanying spirit of proud iconoclasm (with just a hint of asperity) was exemplified by Henry Singleton, in a rare 1979 interview with *Forbes* magazine: "After we acquired a number of businesses, we reflected on business. Our conclusion was that the key was cash flow. . . . Our attitude toward cash generation and asset management came out of our own thinking." He added (as though he needed to), "It is *not* copied."[4]

## CHAPTER 1

# A Perpetual Motion Machine for Returns

## Tom Murphy and Capital Cities Broadcasting

Tom Murphy and Dan Burke were probably the greatest two-person combination in management that the world has ever seen or maybe ever will see.

—*Warren Buffett*

In speaking with business school classes, Warren Buffett often compares the rivalry between Tom Murphy's company, Capital Cities Broadcasting, and CBS to a trans–Atlantic race between a rowboat and the *QE2,* to illustrate the tremendous effect management can have on long–term returns.

When Murphy became the CEO of Capital Cities in 1966, CBS, run by the legendary Bill Paley, was the dominant media business in the country, with TV and radio stations in the country's largest markets, the top-rated broadcast network, and valuable publishing and music properties. In contrast, at that time, Capital Cities had five TV stations and four radio stations, all in smaller markets. CBS's market capitalization was sixteen times the size of Capital Cities'. By the time Murphy sold his company to Disney thirty years later, however, Capital Cities was *three times* as valuable as CBS. In other words, the rowboat had won. Decisively.

So, how did the seemingly insurmountable gap between these two companies get closed? The answer lies in fundamentally different management approaches. CBS spent much of the 1960s and 1970s taking the enormous cash flow generated by its network and broadcast operations and funding an aggressive acquisition program that led it into entirely new fields, including the purchase of a toy business and the New York Yankees baseball team. CBS issued stock to fund some of these acquisitions, built a landmark office building in midtown Manhattan at enormous expense, developed a corporate structure with forty-two presidents and vice presidents, and generally displayed what Buffett's partner, Charlie Munger, calls "a prosperity-blinded indifference to unnecessary costs."[1]

Paley's strategy at CBS was consistent with the conventional wisdom of the conglomerate era, which espoused the elusive benefits of "diversification" and "synergy" to justify the acquisition of unrelated businesses that, once combined with the parent company, would magically become both more profitable and less susceptible to the economic cycle. At its core, Paley's strategy focused on making CBS larger.

In contrast, Murphy's goal was to make his company more valuable. As he said to me, "The goal is not to have the longest train, but to arrive at the station first using the least fuel."[2] Under Murphy and his lieutenant, Dan Burke, Capital Cities rejected diversification and instead created an unusually streamlined conglomerate that focused laser-like on the media businesses it knew well. Murphy acquired more radio and TV stations, operated them superbly well, regularly repurchased his shares, and eventually acquired CBS's rival broadcast network ABC. The relative results speak for themselves.

The formula that allowed Murphy to overtake Paley's *QE2* was deceptively simple: focus on industries with attractive economic characteristics, selectively use leverage to buy occasional large properties, improve operations, pay down debt, and repeat. As Murphy put it succinctly in an interview with *Forbes,* "We just kept opportunistically buying assets, intelligently leveraging the company, improving operations and then we'd . . . take a bite of something else."[3] What's interesting, however, is that his peers at other media companies didn't follow this path. Rather, they tended, like CBS, to follow fashion and diversify into unrelated businesses, build large corporate staffs, and overpay for marquee media properties.

Capital Cities under Murphy was an extremely successful example of what we would now call a *roll-up*. In a typical roll-up, a company acquires a series of businesses, attempts to improve operations, and then keeps acquiring, benefiting over time from scale advantages and best management practices. This concept came into vogue in the mid- to late 1990s and flamed out in the early 2000s as many of the leading companies collapsed under the burden of too much debt. These companies typically failed because they acquired too rapidly and underestimated the difficulty and importance of integrating acquisitions and improving operations.

Murphy's approach to the roll-up was different. He moved slowly, developed real operational expertise, and focused on a small number of large acquisitions that he knew to be high-probability bets. Under Murphy, Capital Cities combined excellence in both operations and capital allocation to an unusual degree. As Murphy told me, "The business of business is a lot of little decisions every day mixed up with a few big decisions."

. . .

Tom Murphy was born in 1925 in Brooklyn, New York. He served in the navy in World War II, graduated from Cornell on the GI Bill, and was a prominent member of the legendary Harvard Business School (HBS) class of 1949 (whose graduates included a future SEC chairman and numerous successful entrepreneurs and *Fortune* 500 CEOs). After graduation from HBS, Murphy worked as a product manager for consumer packaged goods giant Lever Brothers. Ironically (since he's a teetotaler), his life changed irrevocably when he attended a summer cocktail party in 1954 at his parents' home in Schenectady, New York. His father, a prominent local judge, had also invited a longtime friend, Frank Smith, the business manager for famed broadcast journalist Lowell Thomas and a serial entrepreneur.

Smith immediately pigeonholed Murphy and began to tell him about his latest venture—WTEN, a struggling UHF TV station in Albany that Smith had just purchased out of bankruptcy. The station was located in an abandoned former convent, and before the evening was over, young Murphy had agreed to leave his prestigious job in New York and relocate to Albany to run it. He had no broadcasting experience nor for that matter any relevant management experience of any kind.

From the outset, Smith managed the business from his office in downtown Manhattan, leaving day-to-day operations largely to Murphy. After a couple of years of operating losses, Murphy turned the station into a consistent cash generator by improving programming and aggressively managing costs, a formula that the company would apply repeatedly in the years ahead. In 1957, Smith and Murphy bought a second station, in Raleigh, North Carolina, this one located in a former sanitarium. After the addition of a third station, in Providence, Rhode Island, the company adopted the name Capital Cities.

In 1961, Murphy hired Dan Burke, a thirty-year-old Harvard MBA—also with no prior broadcast experience—as his replacement at the Albany station. Burke had been originally introduced to Murphy in the late 1950s by his older brother Jim, who was a classmate of Murphy's at HBS and a rising young executive at Johnson & Johnson (he would eventually become CEO and win accolades for his handling of the Tylenol crisis in the mid-1980s). Dan Burke had served in the Korean War and then entered HBS, graduating in the class of 1955. He then joined General Foods as a product manager in the Jell-O division and, in 1961, signed on with Capital Cities, where Murphy quickly indoctrinated him into the company's lean, decentralized operating philosophy, which he would come to exemplify.

Murphy then moved to New York to work with Smith to build the company through acquisition. Over the next four years, under Smith and Murphy's direction, Capital Cities grew by selectively acquiring additional radio and television stations, until Smith's death in 1966.

After Smith's death, Murphy became CEO (at age forty). The company had finished the preceding year with revenue of just $28 million. Murphy's first move was to elevate Burke to the role of president and chief operating officer. Theirs was an excellent partnership with a very clear division of labor: Burke was responsible for daily management of operations, and Murphy for acquisitions, capital allocation, and occasional interaction with Wall Street. As Burke told me, "Our relationship was built on a foundation of mutual respect. I had an appetite for and a willingness to do things that Murphy was not interested in doing." Burke believed his "job was to create the free cash flow and Murphy's was to spend it."[4] He exemplifies the central role played in this book by exceptionally strong COOs whose close oversight of operations allowed their CEO partners to focus on longer-term strategic and capital allocation issues.

Once in the CEO seat, it did not take Murphy long to make his mark. In 1967, he bought KTRK, the Houston ABC affiliate, for $22 million—the largest acquisition in broadcast history up to that time. In 1968, Murphy bought Fairchild Communications, a leading publisher of trade magazines, for $42 million. And in 1970, he made his largest purchase yet with the acquisition of broadcaster Triangle Communications from Walter Annenberg for $120 million. After the Triangle transaction, Capital Cities owned five VHF TV stations, the maximum then allowed by the FCC.

Murphy next turned his attention to newspaper publishing, which, as an advertising-driven business with attractive margins and strong competitive barriers, had close similarities to the broadcasting business. After purchasing several small dailies in the early 1970s, he bought the *Fort Worth Telegram* for $75 million in 1974 and the *Kansas City Star* for $95 million in 1977. In 1980, looking for other growth avenues in related businesses, he entered the nascent cable television business with the purchase of Cablecom for $139 million.

During the extended bear market of the mid-1970s to early 1980s, Murphy became an aggressive purchaser of his own shares, eventually buying in close to 50 percent, most of it at single-digit price-to-earnings (P/E) multiples. In 1984, the FCC relaxed its station ownership rules, and in January 1986, Murphy, in his masterstroke, bought the ABC Network and its related broadcasting assets (including major-market TV stations in New York, Chicago, and Los Angeles) for nearly $3.5 billion with financing from his friend Warren Buffett.

The ABC deal was the largest non−oil and gas transaction in business history to that point and an enormous bet-the-company transaction for Murphy, representing over 100 percent of Capital Cities' enterprise value. The acquisition stunned the media world and was greeted with the headline "Minnow Swallows Whale" in the *Wall Street Journal*. At closing, Burke said to media investor Gordon Crawford, "This is the acquisition I've been training for my whole life."[5]

The core economic rationale for the deal was Murphy's conviction that he could improve the margins for ABC's TV stations from the low thirties up to Capital Cities' industry-leading levels (50-plus percent). Under Burke's oversight, the staff that oversaw ABC's TV station group dropped from sixty to eight, the head count at the flagship WABC station in New York was reduced from six hundred to four hundred, and the margin gap was closed in just two years.

Burke and Murphy wasted little time in implementing Capital Cities' lean, decentralized approach—immediately cutting unnecessary perks, such as the executive elevator and the private dining room, and moving quickly to eliminate redundant positions, laying off fifteen hundred employees in the first several months after the transaction closed. They also consolidated offices and sold off unnecessary real estate, collecting $175 million for the headquarters building in midtown Manhattan. As Bob Zelnick of ABC News said, "After the mid-80s, we stopped flying first class."[6]

A story from this time demonstrates the culture clash between network executives and the leaner, more entrepreneurial acquirers. ABC, in fact the whole broadcasting industry, was a limousine culture—one of the most cherished perks for an industry executive was the ability to take a limo for even a few blocks to lunch. Murphy, however, was a cab man and from very early on showed up to all ABC meetings in cabs. Before long, this practice rippled through the ABC executive ranks, and the broader Capital Cities ethos slowly began to permeate the ABC culture. When asked whether this was a case of leading by example, Murphy responded, "Is there any other way?"

In the nine years after the transaction, revenues and cash flows grew significantly in every major ABC business line, including the TV stations, the publishing assets, and ESPN. Even the network, which had been in last place at the time of the acquisition, was ranked number one in prime time ratings and was more profitable than either CBS or NBC.

Capital Cities never made another large-scale acquisition after the ABC deal, focusing instead on integration, smaller acquisitions, and continued stock repurchases. In 1993, immediately after his sixty-fifth birthday, Burke retired from Capital Cities, surprising even Murphy. (Burke subsequently bought the Portland Sea Dogs baseball team, where he oversaw the rebirth of that franchise, now one of the most respected in the minor leagues.)

In the summer of 1995, Buffett suggested to Murphy that he sit down with Michael Eisner, the CEO of Disney, at the annual Allen & Company gathering of media nabobs in Sun Valley, Idaho. Murphy, who was seventy years old and without an apparent successor, agreed to meet Eisner, who had expressed an interest in buying the company. Over several days, Murphy negotiated an extraordinary $19 billion price for his shareholders, a multiple of 13.5 times cash flow and 28 times net income. Murphy took a seat on Disney's board and subsequently retired from active management.

He left behind an ecstatic group of shareholders—if you had invested a dollar with Tom Murphy as he became CEO in 1966, that dollar would have been worth *$204* by the time he sold the company to Disney. That's a remarkable *19.9 percent* internal rate of return over twenty-nine years, significantly outpacing the 10.1 percent return for the S&P 500 and 13.2 percent return for an index of leading media companies over the same period. (The investment also proved lucrative for Warren Buffett, generating a compound annual return of greater than *20 percent* for Berkshire Hathaway over a ten-year holding period.) As figure 1-1 shows, in his twenty-nine years at Capital Cities, Murphy outperformed the S&P by a phenomenal *16.7 times* and his peers by almost *fourfold*.

**FIGURE 1-1**

## Capital Cities' stock performance

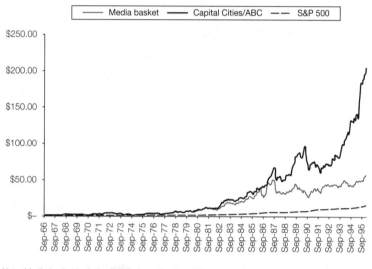

*Note:* Media basket includes Taft Communications (September 1966–April 1986), Metromedia (September 1966–August 1980), Times Mirror (August 1966–January 1995), Cox Communications (September 1966–August 1985), Gannett (March 1969–January 1996), Knight Ridder (August 1969–January 1996), Harte-Hanks (February 1973–September 1984), and Dow Jones (December 1972–January 1996).

## The Nuts and Bolts

One of the major themes in this book is resource allocation.

There are two basic types of resources that any CEO needs to allocate: financial and human. We've touched on the former already. The latter is, however, also critically important, and here again the outsider CEOs shared an unconventional approach, one that emphasized flat organizations and dehydrated corporate staffs.

There is a fundamental humility to decentralization, an admission that headquarters does not have all the answers and that much of the real value is created by local managers in the field. At no company was decentralization more central to the corporate ethos than at Capital Cities.

The hallmark of the company's culture—extraordinary autonomy for operating managers—was stated succinctly in a single paragraph on the inside cover of every Capital Cities annual report: "Decentralization is the cornerstone of our philosophy. Our goal is to hire the best people we can and give them the responsibility and authority they need to perform their jobs. All decisions are made at the local level. . . . We expect our managers . . . to be forever cost conscious and to recognize and exploit sales potential."

Headquarters staff was anorexic, and its primary purpose was to support the general managers of operating units. There were no vice presidents in functional areas like marketing, strategic planning, or human resources; no corporate counsel and no public relations department (Murphy's secretary fielded all calls from the media). In the Capital Cities culture, the publishers and station managers had the power and prestige internally, and they almost never heard from New York if they were hitting their numbers. It was an environment that selected for and promoted independent, entrepreneurial general managers. The company's guiding human resource philosophy, repeated ad infinitum by Murphy, was to "hire the best people you can and leave them alone." As Burke told me, the company's extreme decentralized approach "kept both costs and rancor down."

The guinea pig in the development of this philosophy was Dan Burke himself. In 1961, after he took over as general manager at

WTEN, Burke began sending weekly memos to Murphy as he had been trained to do at General Foods. After several months of receiving no response, he stopped sending them, realizing his time was better spent on local operations than on reporting to headquarters. As Burke said in describing his early years in Albany, "Murphy delegates to the point of anarchy."[7]

Frugality was also central to the ethos. Murphy and Burke realized early on that while you couldn't control your revenues at a TV station, you could control your costs. They believed that the best defense against the revenue lumpiness inherent in advertising-supported businesses was a constant vigilance on costs, which became deeply embedded in the company's culture.

In fact, in one of the earliest and most often told corporate legends, Murphy even scrutinized the company's expenditures on paint. Shortly after Murphy arrived in Albany, Smith asked him to paint the dilapidated former convent that housed the studio to project a more professional image to advertisers. Murphy's immediate response was to paint the two sides facing the road leaving the other sides untouched ("forever cost conscious"). A picture of WTEN still hangs in Murphy's New York office.

Murphy and Burke believed that even the smallest operating decisions, particularly those relating to head count, could have unforeseen long-term costs and needed to be watched constantly. Phil Meek, head of the publishing division, took this message to heart and ran the entire publishing operation (six daily newspapers, several magazine groups, and a stable of weekly shoppers) with only three people at headquarters, including an administrative assistant.

Burke pursued economic efficiency with a zeal that earned him the nickname "The Cardinal." To run the company's dispersed operations, he developed a legendarily detailed annual budgeting process. Each year, every general manager came to New York for extensive budget meetings. In these sessions, management presented operating and capital budgets for the coming year, and Burke and his CFO, Ron Doerfler, went through them in line-by-line detail (interestingly, Burke could be as tough on minority hiring shortfalls as on excessive costs).

The budget sessions were not perfunctory and almost always produced material changes. Particular attention was paid to capital expenditures and expenses. Managers were expected to outperform their peers, and great attention was paid to margins, which Burke viewed as "a form of report card." Outside of these meetings, managers were left alone and sometimes went months without hearing from corporate.

The company did not simply cut its way to high margins, however. It also emphasized investing in its businesses for long-term growth. Murphy and Burke realized that the key drivers of profitability in most of their businesses were revenue growth and advertising market share, and they were prepared to invest in their properties to ensure leadership in local markets.

For example, Murphy and Burke realized early on that the TV station that was number one in local news ended up with a disproportionate share of the market's advertising revenue. As a result, Capital Cities stations always invested heavily in news talent and technology, and remarkably, virtually every one of its stations led in its local market. In another example, Burke insisted on spending substantially more money to upgrade the Fort Worth printing plant than Phil Meek had requested, realizing the importance of color printing in maintaining the *Telegram*'s long-term competitive position. As Phil Beuth, an early employee, told me, "The company was careful, not just cheap."[8]

The company's hiring practices were equally unconventional. With no prior broadcasting experience themselves before joining Capital Cities, Murphy and Burke shared a clear preference for intelligence, ability, and drive over direct industry experience. They were looking for talented, younger foxes with fresh perspectives. When the company made an acquisition or entered a new industry, it inevitably designated a top Capital Cities executive, often from an unrelated division, to oversee the new property. In this vein, Bill James, who had been running the flagship radio property, WJR in Detroit, was tapped to run the cable division, and John Sias, previously head of the publishing division, took over the ABC Network. Neither had any prior industry experience; both produced excellent results.

Murphy and Burke were also comfortable giving responsibility to promising young managers. As Murphy described it to me, "We'd been fortunate enough to have it ourselves and knew it could work." Bill James was thirty-five and had no radio experience when he took over WJR; Phil Meek came over from the Ford Motor Company at thirty-two with no publishing experience to run the *Pontiac Press;* and Bob Iger was thirty-seven and had spent his career in broadcast sports when he moved from New York to Hollywood to assume responsibility for ABC Entertainment.

The company also had exceptionally low turnover. As Robert Price, a rival broadcaster, once remarked, "We always see lots of résumés but we never see any from Capital Cities."[9] Dan Burke related to me a conversation with Frank Smith on the effectiveness of this philosophy. Burke recalls Smith saying, "The system in place corrupts you with so much autonomy and authority that you can't imagine leaving."

. . .

In the area of capital allocation, Murphy's approach was highly differentiated from his peers. He eschewed diversification, paid de minimis dividends, rarely issued stock, made active use of leverage, regularly repurchased shares, and between long periods of inactivity, made the occasional very large acquisition.

The two primary sources of capital for Capital Cities were internal operating cash flow and debt. As we've seen, the company produced consistently high, industry-leading levels of operating cash flow, providing Murphy with a reliable source of capital to allocate to acquisitions, buybacks, debt repayment, and other investment options.

Murphy also frequently used debt to fund acquisitions, once summarizing his approach as "always, we've . . . taken the assets once we've paid them off and leveraged them again to buy other assets."[10] After closing an acquisition, Murphy actively deployed free cash flow to reduce debt levels, and these loans were typically paid down ahead of schedule. The bulk of the ABC debt was retired within three years of the transaction. Interestingly, Murphy never borrowed money to fund a share repurchase, preferring to utilize leverage for the purchase of operating businesses.

Murphy and Burke actively avoided dilution from equity offerings. Other than the sale of stock to Berkshire Hathaway to help finance the ABC acquisition, the company did not issue new stock over the twenty years prior to the Disney sale, and over this period total shares outstanding shrank by 47 percent as a result of repeated repurchases.

Acquisitions were far and away the largest outlet for the company's capital during Murphy's tenure. According to recent studies, somewhere around two-thirds of all acquisitions actually destroy value for shareholders. How then was such enormous value created by acquisitions at Capital Cities? Acquisitions were Murphy's bailiwick and where he spent the majority of his time. He did not delegate acquisition decisions, never used investment bankers, and over time, evolved an idiosyncratic approach that was both effective and different in significant and important ways from his competitors'.

To Murphy, as a capital allocator, the company's extreme decentralization had important benefits: it allowed the company to operate more profitably than its peers (Capital Cities had the highest margins in each of its business lines), which in turn gave the company an advantage in acquisitions by allowing Murphy to buy properties and know that under Burke, they would quickly be made more profitable, lowering the effective price paid. In other words, the company's operating and integration expertise occasionally gave Murphy that scarcest of business commodities: *conviction*.

And when he had conviction, Murphy was prepared to act aggressively. Under his leadership, Capital Cities was extremely acquisitive, three separate times doing the largest deal in the history of the broadcast industry, culminating in the massive ABC transaction. Over this time period, the company was also involved with several of the largest newspaper acquisitions in the country, as well as transactions in the radio, cable TV, and magazine publishing industries.

Murphy was willing to wait a long time for an attractive acquisition. He once said, "I get paid not just to make deals, but to make *good* deals."[11] When he saw something that he liked, however, Murphy was prepared to make a very large bet, and much of the value created during his nearly thirty-year tenure as CEO was the result of a handful of large acquisition decisions, each of which produced excellent long-terms returns. These acquisitions each represented 25 percent or more of the company's market capitalization at the time they were made.

Murphy was a master at prospecting for deals. He was known for his sense of humor and for his honesty and integrity. Unlike other media company CEOs, he stayed out of the public eye (although this became more difficult after the ABC acquisition). These traits helped him as he prospected for potential acquisitions. Murphy knew what he wanted to buy, and he spent years developing relationships with the owners of desirable properties. He never participated in a hostile takeover situation, and *every* major transaction that the company completed was sourced via direct contact with sellers, such as Walter Annenberg of Triangle and Leonard Goldenson of ABC.

He worked hard to become a preferred buyer by treating employees fairly and running properties that were consistent leaders in their markets. This reputation helped him enormously when he approached Goldenson about buying ABC in 1984 (in his typical self-deprecating style, Murphy began his pitch with "Leonard, please don't throw me out the window, but I'd like to buy your company.")

Beneath this avuncular, outgoing exterior, however, lurked a razor-sharp business mind. Murphy was a highly disciplined buyer who had strict return requirements and did not stretch for acquisitions—once missing a very large newspaper transaction involving three Texas properties over a $5 million difference in price. Like others in this book, he relied on simple but powerful rules in evaluating transactions. For Murphy, that benchmark was a double-digit after-tax return over ten years without leverage. As a result of this pricing discipline, he *never* prevailed in an auction, although he participated in many. Murphy told me that his auction bids consistently ended up at only 60 to 70 percent of the eventual transaction price.

Murphy had an unusual negotiating style. He believed in "leaving something on the table" for the seller and said that in the best transactions, everyone came away happy. He would often ask the seller what they thought their property was worth, and if he thought their offer was fair he'd take it (as he did when Annenberg told him the Triangle stations were worth ten times pretax profits). If he thought their proposal was high, he would counter with his best price, and if the seller rejected his offer, Murphy would walk away. He believed this straightforward approach saved time and avoided unnecessary acrimony.

Share repurchases were another important outlet for Murphy, providing him with an important capital allocation benchmark, and he made frequent use of them over the years. When the company's multiple was low relative to private market comparables, Murphy bought back stock. Over the years, Murphy devoted over $1.8 billion to buybacks, mostly at single-digit multiples of cash flow. Collectively, these repurchases represented a very large bet for the company, second in size only to the ABC transaction,

## The Publishing Division

After the Triangle transaction in 1970, Capital Cities was prevented from owning additional TV stations by FCC regulations. As a result, Murphy turned his attention to newspapers and, between 1974 and 1978, initiated the two largest transactions in the industry's history to that time—the acquisition of the *Fort Worth Telegram* and the *Kansas City Star*—as well as the purchase of several smaller daily and weekly newspapers across the United States.

The company's performance in its newspaper publishing division provides an interesting litmus test of its operating skills. Under the leadership of Jim Hale and Phil Meek, Capital Cities evolved an approach to the newspaper business that grew out of its experience in operating TV stations, with an emphasis on careful cost control and maximizing advertising market share.

What is remarkable in looking at the company's four major newspaper operations is the consistent year-after-year-after-year growth in revenues and operating cash flow. Amazingly, these properties, which were sold to Knight Ridder in 1997, collectively produced a 25 percent compound rate of return over an average twenty-year holding period. According to the *Kansas City Star*'s publisher Bob Woodworth (subsequently the CEO of Pulitzer Inc.), the operating margin at the *Star,* the company's largest paper, expanded from the single digits in the mid-1970s to a high of 35 percent in 1996, while cash flow grew from $12.5 million to $68 million.

and they generated excellent returns for shareholders, with a cumulative compound return of 22.4 percent over nineteen years. As Murphy says today, "I only wished I'd bought more."

The phenomenal long-term performance of Capital Cities drew the admiration of the country's top media investors. Warren

## Chronicle Publishing: A Successful Transplant

Capital Cities' distinctive approach to operations and human resources was successfully transplanted to a West Coast media company, Chronicle Publishing, in the mid- to late 1990s by John Sias, the former head of Capital Cities' publishing division and the ABC Network. In 1993, Sias took over as the CEO of Chronicle, a diversified, family-owned media company, headquartered in San Francisco.

Chronicle owned the *San Francisco Chronicle* newspaper, the NBC affiliate in San Francisco (KRON), three hundred thousand cable subscribers, and a book publishing company. Prior to Sias's arrival, the company had been torn by family squabbling, and operations had suffered. Sias and his young CFO, Alan Nichols, wasted no time in implementing the Capital Cities operating model, radically transforming the company's operations. They immediately eliminated an entire layer of executives at corporate headquarters, instituted a rigorous budgeting process, and gave significant authority and autonomy to the general managers (many of whom, uncomfortable in the new, more demanding culture, left in the first year).

The results were stunning. The margins at KRON improved by an incredible 2,000 basis points, from 30 percent to 50 percent (KRON was eventually sold for over $730 million in June 2000), and the operating margins at the *Chronicle* newspaper (which operated under an unusual joint operating agreement with the *San Francisco Examiner*)

Buffett and Mario Gabelli each went back to the legendary Yankee sluggers of their respective eras (Ruth and Gehrig for Buffett, and Mantle and Maris for Gabelli) to find analogies for Murphy and Burke's managerial performance. Gordon Crawford, a shareholder from 1972 until the Disney sale and one of the most more than doubled, from 4 percent to 10 percent (Hearst bought the paper for an astronomical $660 million in 1999). Sias and Nichols also merged the cable subscribers into Tele-Communications Inc. (TCI) in a tax-free exchange and sold the book division at an attractive price to one of the family members. Sias retired from the company in 1999, after having created hundreds of millions of dollars of value for its shareholders.

### The Diaspora

As with the large number of successful NFL coaches who once worked for Bill Walsh or surgeons who worked at the Peter Bent Brigham Hospital in Boston in the 1950s and 1960s under Francis Moore, the media world is littered with Capital Cities alums. The company's culture and operating model were widely admired, and in addition to Sias at Chronicle, former company executives have occupied top management slots at a dizzying variety of media companies, starting with Disney itself (now run by Bob Iger). Capital Cities alums have also held executive positions at LIN Broadcasting (CEO), Pulitzer (CEO), Hearst (CFO), and E. W. Scripps (head of newspaper operations), among others. Dan Burke's son, Steve, formerly COO of Comcast, is now the CEO of NBCUniversal.

influential media investors in the country, believed Murphy and Burke's unique blend of operating and capital allocation skills created a "perpetual motion machine for returns."[12] Capital Cities' admirers also included Bill Ruane of Ruane, Cunniff, and David Wargo of State Street Research.

Although the focus here is on quantifiable business performance, it is worth noting that Murphy built a universally admired company at Capital Cities with an exceptionally strong culture and esprit de corps (at least two different groups of executives still hold regular reunions). The company was widely respected by employees, advertisers, and community leaders, in addition to Wall Street analysts. Phil Meek told me a story about a bartender at one of the management retreats who made a handsome return by buying Capital Cities stock in the early 1970s. When an executive later asked why he had made the investment, the bartender replied, "I've worked at a lot of corporate events over the years, but Capital Cities was the only company where you couldn't tell who the bosses were."[13]

## Transdigm: A Contemporary Doppelgänger

A contemporary analog for Capital Cities can be found in Transdigm, a little-known, publicly traded aerospace components manufacturer. This remarkable company has grown its cash flow at a compound rate of *over 25 percent* since 1993 through a combination of internal growth and an exceptionally effective acquisition program. Like Capital Cities, the company focuses on a very specific type of business with exceptional economic characteristics.

In Transdigm's case, this area of specialization is highly engineered aviation parts and components. These parts, once engineered into a military or commercial aircraft, cannot be easily replaced and require regular maintenance and replacement. They are critical to the performance of the aircraft and have no substitutes, and their cost is insignificant relative to the overall cost of the aircraft. As a result, their customers—the largest military and commercial aircraft manufacturers—are more focused on performance than price, and the company has an attractive combination of pricing power and phenomenal margins (cash flow [defined as EBITDA, or earnings before interest, taxes, depreciation, and amortization] margins are north of 40 percent).

Transdigm's management team, led by CEO Nick Howley, realized these excellent economic characteristics in the early 1990s and evolved a highly decentralized corporate structure and operating system for optimizing the profitability of these specialized-parts businesses. Howley, like Murphy at Capital Cities, knows that his team will be able to quickly and dramatically improve the profitability of acquired companies, lowering the effective purchase price paid and providing a compelling logic for future acquisitions.

Since going public, the company has also pursued an unusual and aggressive capital allocation strategy (one that has caused a fair amount of comment and confusion on Wall Street), maintaining generally high levels of leverage, repurchasing shares, and announcing a large special dividend (financed with debt) in the depths of the recent financial crisis. Not surprisingly, returns for the shareholders have also been excellent—the stock has appreciated over fourfold since the company's 2006 initial public offering.

# 2

# An Unconventional Conglomerateur

*Henry Singleton and Teledyne*

Henry Singleton has the best operating and capital deployment record in American business . . . if one took the 100 top business school graduates and made a composite of their triumphs, their record would not be as good as Singleton's.

—*Warren Buffett, 1980*

I change my mind when the facts change. What do you do?

—*John Maynard Keynes*

In early 1987, Teledyne, a midsize conglomerate with a reputation for unconventional behavior, declared a dividend. This seemingly innocuous event attracted inordinate attention in the business press, including a front-page article in the *Wall Street Journal*. What did the *Journal* find so newsworthy?

For most of the twentieth century, public companies were expected to pay out a portion of their annual profits as dividends. Many investors, particularly senior citizens, relied on these dividends for income and looked closely at dividend levels and policies in making investment decisions. Teledyne, however, alone among 1960s–era conglomerates, steadfastly refused to pay dividends, believing them to be tax inefficient (dividends are taxed twice—once at the corporate level and again at the individual level).

In fact, under its reclusive founder and CEO, Henry Singleton, this dividend policy was, as we've seen, just one in a series of highly unusual and contrarian practices at Teledyne. In addition to eschewing dividends, Singleton ran a notoriously decentralized operation; avoided interacting with Wall Street analysts; didn't split his stock; and repurchased his shares as no one else ever has, before or since.

All of this was highly unusual and idiosyncratic, but what really set Singleton apart and eventually made him a Garbo-like legend was his returns, which dwarfed both the market and his conglomerate peers. Singleton managed to grow values at an extraordinary rate across almost thirty years of wildly varying macroeconomic conditions, starting in the "go-go" stock market of the 1960s and ending in the deep bear market of the early 1990s.

He did this by continually adapting to changing market conditions and by maintaining a dogged focus on capital allocation. His approach differed significantly from his peers, and the seeds of this iconoclasm can be traced to his background, which was highly unusual for a *Fortune* 500 CEO.

. . .

Born in 1916 in tiny Haslet, Texas, Singleton was a highly accomplished mathematician and scientist who never earned an MBA. Instead, he attended MIT, where he earned bachelor's, master's, and PhD degrees in electrical engineering. Singleton programmed the first student computer at MIT as part of his doctoral thesis, and in 1939 won the Putnam Medal as the top mathematics student in the country (future winners would include the Nobel Prize–winning physicist Richard Feynman). He was also an avid chess player who was 100 points shy of the grandmaster level.

After graduation from MIT in 1950, he worked as a research engineer at North American Aviation and Hughes Aircraft. He was then recruited by the legendary former Whiz Kid Tex Thornton, to Litton Industries, where, in the late 1950s, he invented an inertial guidance system that is still used in commercial and military aircraft. Singleton was promoted to general manager of Litton's Electronic Systems Group, and under his leadership that division grew to be the company's largest, with over $80 million in revenue by the end of the decade.

Singleton left Litton in 1960 after it became clear to him that he would not succeed Thornton as CEO. He was forty-three years old. His colleague, George Kozmetzky, who ran Litton's Electronic Components Group, left with him, and together, in July 1960, they founded Teledyne. They started by acquiring three small electronics companies, and using this base, they successfully bid for a large naval contract. Teledyne became a public company in 1961 at the dawn of the conglomerate era.

Conglomerates, companies with many, unrelated business units, were the Internet stocks of their day. Taking advantage of their stratospheric stock prices, they grew by voraciously and often indiscriminately acquiring businesses in a wide range of industries. These purchases initially brought higher profits, which led to still higher stock prices that were then used to buy more companies. Most conglomerates built up large corporate headquarters staffs in the belief that they could find and exploit synergies across their disparate companies, and they actively courted Wall Street and the press in order to boost their stock. Their halcyon days, however, came to an abrupt end in the late 1960s when the largest of them (ITT, Litton Industries, and so on) began to miss earnings estimates and their stock prices fell precipitously.

The conventional wisdom today is that conglomerates are an inefficient form of corporate organization, lacking the agility and focus of "pure play" companies. It was not always so—for most of the 1960s, conglomerates enjoyed lofty price-to-earnings (P/E) ratios and used the currency of their high-priced stock to engage in a prolonged frenzy of acquisition. During this heady period, there was significantly less competition for acquisitions than today (private equity firms did not yet exist), and the price to buy control of an operating company (measured by its P/E ratio) was often materially less than the multiple the acquirer traded for in the stock market, providing a compelling logic for acquisitions.

Singleton took full advantage of this extended arbitrage opportunity to develop a diversified portfolio of businesses, and between 1961 and 1969, he purchased *130* companies in industries ranging from aviation electronics to specialty metals and insurance. All but two of these companies were acquired using Teledyne's pricey stock.

Singleton's approach to acquisitions, however, differed from that of other conglomerateurs. He did not buy indiscriminately, avoiding turnaround situations, and focusing instead on profitable, growing companies with leading market positions, often in niche markets. As Jack Hamilton, who ran Teledyne's specialty metals division, summarized his business to me, "We specialized in high-margin products that were sold by the ounce, not the ton."[1] Singleton was a very disciplined buyer, never paying more than twelve times earnings and purchasing most companies at significantly lower multiples. This compares to the high P/E multiple on Teledyne's stock, which ranged from a low of 20 to a high of 50 over this period.

In 1967, in his largest acquisition to date, Singleton acquired Vasco Metals for $43 million and elevated its president, George Roberts, to the role of president of Teledyne, taking the titles of CEO and chairman for himself. Roberts had been Singleton's roommate at the Naval Academy, where he had been admitted at age sixteen as the youngest freshman in the school's history (before both he and Singleton transferred due to Depression-era tuition aid cuts). Roberts also had a scientific background, having graduated from Carnegie Mellon with a PhD in metallurgy before holding a series of executive positions at various specialty metals companies, eventually joining Vasco in the early 1960s as president.

Once Roberts joined the company, Singleton began to remove himself from operations, freeing up the majority of his time to focus on strategic and capital allocation issues.

Shortly thereafter, Singleton became the first of the conglomerateurs to stop acquiring. In mid-1969, with the multiple on his stock falling and acquisition prices rising, he abruptly dismissed his acquisition team. Singleton, as a disciplined buyer, realized that with a lower P/E ratio, the currency of his stock was no longer attractive for acquisitions. From this point on, the company never made another material purchase and never issued another share of stock.

The effectiveness of this acquisition strategy can be seen in table 2-1. Over its first ten years as a public company, Teledyne's earnings per share (EPS) grew an astonishing *sixty-four-fold*, while shares outstanding grew less than fourteen times, resulting in significant value creation for shareholders.

TABLE 2-1

### Teledyne's first-decade financial results ($ in millions)

|  | 1961 | 1971 | Change |
| --- | --- | --- | --- |
| Sales | $4.5 | $1,101.9 | 244.4 times |
| Net income | $0.1 | $32.3 | 555.8 times |
| Earnings per share[a] | $0.13 | $8.55 | 64.8 times |
| Shares outstanding[a] | 0.4 | 6.6 | 13.7 times |
| Debt | $5.1 | $151.0 | 28.9 times |

*Source:* This table was provided by Tom Smith, an investor and longtime Teledyne observer.

a. Adjusted for stock splits and stock dividends.

Singleton came of age at a time when there was great faith in quantitative expertise. The 1940s and 1950s were the era of the "Whiz Kids," a group of exceptionally talented young mathematicians and engineers who used advanced statistical analysis to transform a succession of iconic American institutions, starting with the Army Air Corps (precursor to the modern air force) in World War II, continuing with the Ford Motor Company during the 1950s, and culminating in the Pentagon with the naming of former Whiz Kid Robert McNamara as defense secretary in 1961.

The power in these organizations lay at headquarters with an elite corps of young, exceptionally bright, quantitatively adept executives who exerted centralized control and put new, mathematically based systems in place for running operations. Analytical talent imposed order on far-flung, chaotic operations, resulting in greater efficiency, whether of bombing raids or manufacturing plants.

Many conglomerateurs adopted this headquarters-centric approach to running their companies and developed large corporate staffs, replete with vice presidents and planning departments. Interestingly, Singleton, who had worked closely with Tex Thornton, one of the original Whiz Kids, devised an entirely different approach for his company.

In contrast to peers like Thornton and Harold Geneen at ITT, Singleton and Roberts eschewed the then trendy concepts of "integration" and "synergy" and instead emphasized extreme decentralization, breaking the company into its smallest component parts and driving accountability and managerial responsibility as far down into the organization as possible. At headquarters, there were fewer than fifty people in a company with over forty thousand total employees and no human resource, investor relations, or business development departments. Ironically, the most successful conglomerate of the era was actually the least conglomerate-like in its operations.

This decentralization fostered an objective, apolitical culture at Teledyne. Several former company presidents mentioned this refreshing lack of politics—managers who made their numbers did well; those who did not, moved on. As one told me, "No one worried who Henry was having lunch with."

. . .

Once the acquisition engine had slowed in 1969, Roberts and Singleton turned their attention to the company's existing operations. In another departure from conventional wisdom, Singleton eschewed reported earnings, the key metric on Wall Street at the time, running his company instead to optimize free cash flow. He and his CFO, Jerry Jerome, devised a unique metric that they termed the *Teledyne return,* which by averaging cash flow and net income for each business unit, emphasized cash generation and became the basis for bonus compensation for all business unit general managers. As he once told *Financial World* magazine, "If anyone wants to follow Teledyne, they should get used to the fact that our quarterly earnings will jiggle. Our accounting is set to maximize cash flow, not reported earnings."[2] Not a quote you're likely to hear from the typical Wall Street–focused *Fortune* 500 CEO today.

Singleton and Roberts quickly improved margins and dramatically reduced working capital at Teledyne's operations, generating

## Packard Bell: A Rare Misstep

One division that did not meet Singleton's exacting standards was the Packard Bell television set manufacturing business, and it is interesting to see how he and Roberts handled this rare underperforming business unit. When they realized that Packard Bell had a permanent competitive disadvantage relative to its lower-cost Japanese competitors and could no longer earn acceptable returns, they immediately closed it, becoming the first American manufacturer to exit the industry (all the others followed over the next decade).

---

significant cash in the process. The results can be seen in the consistently high return on assets for Teledyne's operating businesses, which averaged north of 20 percent throughout the 1970s and 1980s. Warren Buffett's partner, Charlie Munger, describes these extraordinary results as "miles higher than anybody else . . . utterly ridiculous."[3]

The net result of these initiatives was that, starting in 1970, the company generated remarkably consistent profitability across a wide variety of market conditions. This influx of cash was sent to headquarters to be allocated by Singleton. The decisions he made in deploying this capital were, not surprisingly, highly unusual (and effective).

. . .

In early 1972, with his cash balance growing and acquisition multiples still high, Singleton placed a call from a midtown Manhattan phone booth to one of his board members, the legendary venture capitalist Arthur Rock (who would later back both Apple and Intel). Singleton began: "Arthur, I've been thinking about it and our stock is simply too cheap. I think we can earn a better return buying our shares at these levels than by doing almost anything else. I'd like to announce a tender—what do you think?" Rock reflected a moment and said, "I like it."[4]

With those words, one of the seminal moments in the history of capital allocation was launched. Starting with that 1972 tender and continuing for the next twelve years, Singleton went on an unprecedented share repurchasing spree that had a galvanic effect on Teledyne's stock price while also almost single-handedly overturning long-held Wall Street beliefs.

To say Singleton was a pioneer in the field of share repurchases is to dramatically understate the case. It is perhaps more accurate to describe him as the Babe Ruth of repurchases, the towering, Olympian figure from the early history of this branch of corporate finance. Prior to the early 1970s, stock buybacks were uncommon and controversial. The conventional wisdom was that repurchases signaled a lack of internal investment opportunity, and they were thus regarded by Wall Street as a sign of weakness. Singleton ignored this orthodoxy, and between 1972 and 1984, in eight separate tender offers, he bought back an astonishing 90 percent of Teledyne's outstanding shares. As Munger says, "No one has ever bought in shares as aggressively."[5]

Singleton believed repurchases were a far more tax-efficient method for returning capital to shareholders than dividends, which for most of his tenure were taxed at very high rates. Singleton believed buying stock at attractive prices was self-catalyzing, analogous to coiling a spring that at some future point would surge forward to realize full value, generating exceptional returns in the process. These repurchases provided a useful capital alloca-tion benchmark, and whenever the return from purchasing his stock looked attractive relative to other investment opportunities, Singleton tendered for his shares.

Repurchases became popular in the 1990s and have frequently been used by CEOs in recent years to prop up sagging stock prices. Buybacks, however, add value for shareholders only if they are made at attractive prices. Not surprisingly, Singleton bought extremely well, generating an incredible 42 percent compound annual return for Teledyne's shareholders across the tenders.

These tender offers were in almost every case oversubscribed. Singleton had done the analysis and knew these buybacks were compelling, and with the strength of his conviction always bought all shares offered. These repurchases were very large bets for Teledyne, ranging in size from 4 percent to an unbelievable 66 percent of the company's book value at the time they were announced. In all, Singleton spent an incredible $2.5 billion on the buybacks.

Table 2-2 puts this achievement in perspective. From 1971 to 1984, Singleton bought back huge chunks of Teledyne's stock at low P/Es while revenues and net income continued to grow, re-sulting in an astonishing *fortyfold* increase in earnings per share.

It's important, however, to recognize that this obsession with repurchases represented an evolution in thinking for Singleton, who, earlier in his career when he was building Teledyne, had been an active and highly effective *issuer* of stock. Great investors (and capital allocators) must be able to both sell high and buy low; the average price-to-earnings ratio for Teledyne's stock issuances

TABLE 2-2

**Results produced by Teledyne's stock repurchase program ($ in millions)**

|  | 1971 | 1984 | Change |
|---|---|---|---|
| Sales | $1,101.9 | $3,494.3 | 2.2 times |
| Net income | $32.3 | $260.7 | 7.1 times |
| Earnings per share[a] | $8.55 | $353.34 | 40.3 times |
| Shares outstanding[a] | 6.6 | 0.9 | (0.9 times) |
| Debt | $151.0 | $1,072.7 | 6.1 times |

*Source:* This table was provided by Tom Smith, an investor and longtime Teledyne observer.

a. Adjusted for stock splits and stock dividends.

was over 25; in contrast, the average multiple for his repurchases was under 8.

. . .

Singleton had been fascinated by the stock market since his teens. George Roberts told me a story of Singleton on leave in New York during World War II standing at the window of a brokerage firm for hours, watching the scroll of stock prices go by on ticker tape.

In the mid-1970s, Singleton finally had an opportunity to act on this lifelong fascination when he assumed direct responsibility for investing the stock portfolios at Teledyne's insurance subsidiaries during a severe bear market with P/E ratios at their lowest levels since the Depression. In the area of portfolio management, as with acquisitions, operations, and repurchases, Singleton developed an idiosyncratic approach with excellent results.

In a significant contrarian move, he aggressively reallocated the assets in these insurance portfolios, increasing the total equity allocation from 10 percent in 1975 to a remarkable 77 percent by 1981. Singleton's approach to implementing this dramatic portfolio shift was even more unusual. He invested over 70 percent of the combined equity portfolios in just five companies, with an incredible 25 percent allocated to one company (his former employer, Litton Industries). This extraordinary portfolio concentration (a typical mutual fund owns over one hundred stocks) caused consternation on Wall Street, where many observers thought Singleton was preparing for a new round of acquisitions.

Singleton had no such intention, but it is instructive to look more closely at how he invested these portfolios. His top holdings were invariably companies he knew well (including smaller conglomerates like Curtiss-Wright and large energy and insurance companies like Texaco and Aetna), whose P/E ratios were at or near record lows at the time of his investment. As Charlie Munger said of Singleton's investment approach, "Like Warren and me, he was comfortable with concentration and bought only a few things that he understood well."[6]

As with his repurchases of Teledyne stock, Singleton's returns in these insurance portfolios were excellent. A proxy for these returns can be seen in figure 2-1, which shows the approximately eightfold growth in book value at Teledyne's insurance subsidiaries from 1975 through 1985, when Singleton began the process of dismantling his company.

During the period from 1984 to 1996, Singleton shifted his focus from portfolio management to management succession (in 1986, he tapped Roberts to succeed him as CEO, retaining the

FIGURE 2-1

**Teledyne insurance book value ($ in millions)[a]**

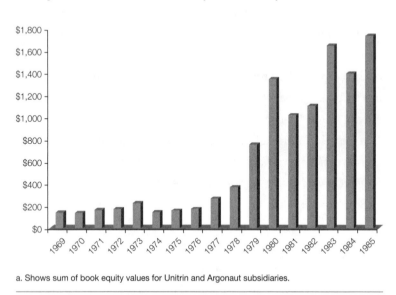

a. Shows sum of book equity values for Unitrin and Argonaut subsidiaries.

chairman's title) and to optimizing shareholder value in the face of stagnating results at Teledyne's operating divisions. To accomplish these objectives, Singleton resorted to new tactics, again confounding Wall Street.

Singleton was a pioneer in the use of spin-offs, which he believed would both simplify succession issues at Teledyne (by reducing the company's complexity) and unlock the full value of the company's large insurance operations for shareholders. In the words of longtime board member Fayez Sarofim, Singleton believed "there was a time to conglomerate and a time to deconglomerate."[7] The time for deconglomeration finally arrived in 1986 with the debut spin-off of Argonaut, the company's worker's compensation insurer.

Next, in 1990, Singleton spun off Unitrin, the company's largest insurance operation, with Jerry Jerome as CEO. This was a significant move as Unitrin accounted for the majority of Teledyne's enterprise value at that time. It has had excellent returns since going public under the leadership of Jerome and his successor, Dick Vie.

Starting in the mid- to late 1980s, Teledyne's noninsurance operations slowed in the face of a cyclical downturn in the energy and specialty metals markets and fraud charges at its defense business. In 1987, at a time when both acquisition and stock prices (including his own) were at historic highs, Singleton concluded that he had no better, higher-returning options for deploying the company's cash flow, and declared the company's first dividend in twenty-six years as a public company. This was a seismic event for longtime Teledyne observers, signaling the arrival of a new phase in the company's history.

After these successful spin-offs and with Roberts established in the CEO role, Singleton retired as chairman in 1991 to focus on his extensive cattle ranching operations. (Ranching held a singular appeal for Singleton as it did for many successful, Texas-born entrepreneurs of his generation, and he would eventually acquire over 1 million acres of ranchland across New Mexico, Arizona, and California.) He returned, however, in 1996 to personally negotiate the merger of Teledyne's remaining manufacturing operations with Allegheny Industries and fend off a hostile takeover bid by raider Bennett LeBow. In these negotiations, according to Bill Rutledge, Teledyne's president at the time, Singleton focused exclusively on getting the best possible price, ignoring other peripheral issues such as management titles and board composition.[8] Again, the outcome was a favorable one for Teledyne shareholders: a 30 percent premium to the company's prior trading price.

Singleton left behind an extraordinary record, dwarfing both his peers and the market. From 1963 (the first year for which we have reliable stock data) to 1990, when he stepped down as chairman, Singleton delivered a remarkable *20.4 percent* compound annual return to his shareholders (including spin-offs), compared to an 8.0 percent return for the S&P 500 over the same period and an 11.6 percent return for other major conglomerate stocks (see figure 2-2).

A dollar invested with Henry Singleton in 1963 would have been worth *$180.94* by 1990, an almost *ninefold* outperformance

**FIGURE 2-2**

### Teledyne stock price during the Singleton era versus S&P 500 and peers

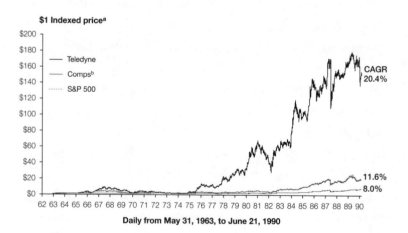

Daily from May 31, 1963, to June 21, 1990

a. Adjusted for stock splits, stock dividends, and cash dividends (assumed to be reinvested and taxed at 40 percent).
b. Comparable conglomerates include Litton Industries, ITT, Gulf & Western, and Textron.

versus his peers and a more than *twelvefold* outperformance versus the S&P 500, leaving Jack Welch a distant speck in his rearview mirror.

## The Nuts and Bolts

One of the most important decisions any CEO makes is how he spends his time—specifically, how much time he spends in three essential areas: management of operations, capital allocation, and investor relations. Henry Singleton's approach to time management was, not surprisingly, very different from peers like Tex Thornton and Harold Geneen and very similar to his fellow outsider CEOs.

As he told *Financial World* magazine in 1978, "I don't reserve *any* day-to-day responsibilities for myself, so I don't get into any particular rut. I do not define my job in any rigid terms but in terms of having the freedom to do whatever seems to be in the best interests of the company at any time."[9] Singleton eschewed detailed strategic plans, preferring instead to retain flexibility and keep options open. As he once explained at a Teledyne annual meeting, "I know a lot of people have very strong and definite plans that they've worked out on all kinds of things, but we're subject to a tremendous number of outside influences and the vast majority of them cannot be predicted. So my idea is to stay flexible."[10] In a rare interview with a *BusinessWeek* reporter, he explained himself more simply: "My only plan is to keep coming to work. . . . I like to steer the boat each day rather than plan ahead way into the future."[11]

Unlike conglomerate peers such as Thornton or Geneen or Gulf & Western's colorful Charles Bluhdorn, Singleton did not

## Teledyne Versus Sarbanes-Oxley

Teledyne's iconoclasm extended to today's hot-button topic of corporate governance. The company's board would fail miserably by the current standards of Sarbanes-Oxley legislation. Singleton (like many of the CEOs in this book) was a proponent of small boards. Teledyne's board consisted of only six directors, including Singleton, half of them insiders. It was an exceptionally talented group, however, and each member had a significant economic interest in the company. In addition to Singleton, Roberts, and Kozmetzky (who retired from Teledyne in 1966 to run the business school at the University of Texas), board members included Claude Shannon, Singleton's MIT classmate and the father of information theory; Arthur Rock, the legendary venture capitalist; and Fayez Sarofim, the billionaire Houston-based fund manager. This group collectively owned almost 40 percent of the company's stock by the end of the period.

court Wall Street analysts or the business press. In fact, he believed investor relations was an inefficient use of time, and simply refused to provide quarterly earnings guidance or appear at industry conferences. This was highly unconventional behavior at a time when his more accommodating peers were often on the cover of the top business magazines.

. . .

Even in a book filled with CEOs who were aggressive in buying back stock, Singleton is in a league of his own. Given his voracious appetite for Teledyne's shares and the overall high levels of repurchases among the outsider CEOs, it's worth looking a little more closely at Singleton's approach to buybacks, which differed significantly from that of most CEOs today.

Fundamentally, there are two basic approaches to buying back stock. In the most common contemporary approach, a company authorizes an amount of capital (usually a relatively small percentage of the excess cash on its balance sheet) for the repurchase of shares and then gradually over a period of quarters (or sometimes years) buys in stock on the open market. This approach is careful, conservative, and, not coincidentally, unlikely to have any meaningful impact on long-term share values. Let's call this cautious, methodical approach the "straw."

The other approach, the one favored by the CEOs in this book and pioneered by Singleton, is quite a bit bolder. This approach features less frequent and much larger repurchases timed to coincide with low stock prices—typically made within very short periods of time, often via tender offers, and occasionally funded with debt. Singleton, who employed this approach no fewer than eight times, disdained the "straw," preferring instead a "suction hose."

Singleton's 1980 share buyback provides an excellent example of his capital allocation acumen. In May of that year, with Teledyne's P/E multiple near an all-time low, Singleton initiated the company's largest tender yet, which was oversubscribed by three-fold. Singleton decided to buy all the tendered shares (*over 20 percent* of shares outstanding), and given the company's strong free cash flow and a recent drop in interest rates, financed the entire repurchase with fixed-rate debt.

After the repurchase, interest rates rose sharply, and the price of the newly issued bonds fell. Singleton did not believe interest rates were likely to continue to rise, so he initiated a buyback of the bonds. He retired the bonds, however, with cash from the company's pension fund, which was not taxed on investment gains.

As a result of this complex series of transactions, Teledyne successfully financed a large stock repurchase with inexpensive debt, the pension fund realized sizable tax-free gains on its bond purchase when interest rates subsequently fell, and, oh yes . . . the stock appreciated enormously (a ten-year compound return of *over 40 percent*).

. . .

Singleton's fierce independence of mind remained a prominent trait until the end of his life. In 1997, two years before his death from brain cancer at age eighty-two, he sat down with Leon Cooperman, a longtime Teledyne investor. At the time, a number of *Fortune* 500 companies had recently announced large share repurchases. When Cooperman asked him about them, Singleton responded presciently, "If everyone's doing them, there must be something wrong with them."[12]

## Buffett and Singleton: Separated at Birth?

Many of the distinctive tenets of Warren Buffett's unique approach to managing Berkshire Hathaway were first employed by Singleton at Teledyne. In fact, Singleton can be seen as a sort of proto-Buffett, and there are uncanny similarities between these two virtuoso CEOs, as the following list demonstrates.

- *The CEO as investor.* Both Buffett and Singleton designed organizations that allowed them to focus on capital allocation, not operations. Both viewed themselves primarily as investors, not managers.

- *Decentralized operations, centralized investment decisions.* Both ran highly decentralized organizations with very few employees at corporate and few, if any, intervening layers between operating companies and top management. Both made all major capital allocation decisions for their companies.

- *Investment philosophy.* Both Buffett and Singleton focused their investments in industries they knew well, and were comfortable with concentrated portfolios of public securities.

- *Approach to investor relations.* Neither offered quarterly guidance to analysts or attended conferences. Both provided informative annual reports with detailed business unit information.

- *Dividends.* Teledyne, alone among conglomerates, didn't pay a dividend for its first twenty-six years. Berkshire has never paid a dividend.

- *Stock splits.* Teledyne was the highest-priced issue on the NYSE for much of the 1970s and 1980s. Buffett has never split Berkshire's A shares (which now trade at over $120,000 a share).

- *Significant CEO ownership.* Both Singleton and Buffett had significant ownership stakes in their companies (13 percent for Singleton and 30-plus percent for Buffet). They thought like owners because they *were* owners.

- *Insurance subsidiaries.* Both Singleton and Buffett recognized the potential to invest insurance company "float" to create shareholder value, and for both companies, insurance was the largest and most important business.

- *The restaurant analogy.* Phil Fisher, a famous investor, once compared companies to restaurants—over time through a combination of policies and decisions (analogous to cuisine, prices, and ambiance), they self-select for a certain clientele. By this standard, both Buffett and Singleton intentionally ran highly unusual restaurants that over time attracted like-minded, long-term-oriented customer/ shareholders.

3

# The Turnaround

*Bill Anders and General Dynamics*

A foolish consistency is the hobgoblin of little minds.

—*Ralph Waldo Emerson*

In 1989, after nearly thirty years as the international symbol of Cold War tension and anxiety, the Berlin Wall came down, and, with its fall, the US defense industry's longtime business model also crumbled. The industry had traditionally relied on selling the large weapons systems (missiles, bombers, and so forth) that were the backbone of US post–World War II military strategy. As the decades-long policy of Soviet containment became seemingly obsolete overnight, the industry was thrust into turmoil. Long seen as a cozy fraternity of former generals and admirals, the industry's leading executives scrambled to redefine their companies. Within six months of the Wall's demise, an index of the leading publicly traded defense companies had fallen 40 percent. One company seemed particularly poorly positioned.

General Dynamics had been a pioneer in the defense industry. The company traced its roots back to the late nineteenth century and had a long history selling major weapons to the Pentagon, including aircraft (both the legendary B-29 bomber during WWII and the F-16 fighter plane, workhorse of the modern air force), ships (as the leading manufacturer of submarines), and land vehicles (as the leading supplier of tanks and other combat vehicles). Over the years, the company had diversified into missiles and space systems and a number of nondefense businesses, including Cessna commercial planes and building supplies. General Dynamics had been wracked by scandal in the 1980s as federal investigators discovered abuse of company planes and other perquisites by top executives.

In 1986, the company brought in a new CEO, Stan Pace, with an excellent reputation at the Pentagon. Pace improved relations with the Joint Chiefs of Staff, but operations stagnated, and in 1990 the company learned of the potential cancellation of its largest new aircraft program, the A-12. When a new CEO took over in January 1991, General Dynamics had $600 million of debt and negative cash flow, and faced conjecture about a possible bankruptcy. The company had revenues of $10 billion and a market capitalization of just $1 billion. In the words of Goldman Sachs's defense analyst Judy Bollinger, the company was the "lowest of the low," the worst-positioned company in a declining industry.[1]

In other words, this was a turnaround. Companies in financial distress often hire restructuring "consultants" who helicopter in, slash costs, negotiate with lenders and suppliers, and look to sell the company as quickly as possible before moving on to the next assignment. These hired guns tend to ignore longer-term considerations like culture, capital investment, and organizational structure, focusing instead on short-term cash needs. Turnarounds often succeed in generating attractive near-term returns, usually concluding with the sale of the business to a larger company, a process that has been likened to taking the last puffs from a cigar butt.

It is unusual for a turnaround to sustain high returns over long periods of time and across multiple CEOs, which is exactly what happened at General Dynamics. The General Dynamics story shows how the key elements of the approach used by the outsider CEOs can be effective even in situations of significant industry dislocation.

. . .

It all began when Bill Anders assumed the helm at General Dynamics in January 1991, at the depth of the early 1990s, post–Gulf War bear market. Anders was definitely not your garden-variety CEO. He had had a remarkably distinguished, if unconventional, career before he joined General Dynamics, graduating with an electrical engineering degree from the Naval Academy in 1955 and serving as an air force fighter pilot during the Cold War. He earned an advanced degree in nuclear engineering in 1963 and was one of only fourteen men chosen from a pool of thousands to join NASA's elite astronaut corps.

As the lunar module pilot on the 1968 Apollo 8 mission, Anders took the now-iconic *Earthrise* photograph, which eventually appeared on the covers of *Time, Life,* and *American Photography*. A leading defense analyst believes these early accomplishments gave Anders the ability to take risks in later pursuits: "After orbiting the moon, mundane business problems did not faze him."

He left NASA with the rank of major general and was named the first chairman of the Nuclear Regulatory Commission before serving a brief stint as ambassador to Norway, all before the age of forty-five. He was well known and respected at the Pentagon, and after leaving the public sector, he joined General Electric, where he trained in the GE management approach and was a contemporary of Jack Welch's. As he says, "There was a terrific group of GE managers who were excellent swimming instructors . . . although they occasionally tried to drown you."[2]

Anders was eventually hired in 1984 to run the commercial operations of pioneering conglomerate Textron Corporation, an experience he found frustrating. He had an independent, contrarian personality and a direct-to-the-point-of-bluntness communications style. Not impressed with Textron's eclectic mix of generally mediocre businesses and bureaucratic corporate structure, he, not surprisingly, clashed with Textron's incumbent CEO.

In 1989, he met a senior General Dynamics executive at a trade association meeting, and when offered the chance to join the company as vice-chairman for a year and then move into the CEO slot, he leapt at the opportunity. He spent that interim period getting to know the company's businesses and culture and studying, with the assistance of Bain & Company, the massive changes roiling the industry as the era of lofty defense spending came to a seemingly abrupt halt. This year of study enabled him to hit the ground running when he was formally named CEO.

Although he is the oldest CEO in this book and the only one to take the helm in his fifties, Anders had only ten years of private sector experience when he accepted the General Dynamics post, and his eyes were still very fresh.

The defense industry, traditionally run by engineers and retired military brass, had something of the feel of a club or fraternity. Anders, both an engineer and a former general, was uniquely positioned to take a broom to the industry's cobwebs, and his conclusions (and subsequent actions) would shake the cozy defense community to its core.

. . .

His turnaround strategy for General Dynamics was rooted in a central strategic insight: the defense industry had significant excess capacity following the end of the Cold War. As a result, Anders believed industry players needed to move aggressively to either shrink their businesses or grow through acquisition. In this new environment, there would be consolidators and consolidatees, and companies needed to figure out quickly which camp they belonged in. Anders outlined his strategy in his initial annual and quarterly reports and proceeded to aggressively implement it.

This strategy rested on three key tenets:

1. Anders, borrowing a page from his former GE colleague Welch, believed General Dynamics should only be in businesses where it had the number one or number two market position. (This was strikingly similar to the Powell Doctrine of the same era, which called for the United States to only enter military conflicts that it could win decisively.)

2. The company would exit commodity businesses where returns were unacceptably low.

3. It would stick to businesses it knew well. Specifically, it would be wary of commercial businesses—long an elusive, holy grail–like source of new profits for defense companies.

The company would exit businesses that did not meet these strategic criteria.

Additionally, Anders believed that General Dynamics needed dramatic cultural change. As he conducted thorough interviews with top executives prior to becoming CEO, he found a deeply ingrained engineering mind-set with a relentless focus on the development of "larger, faster, more lethal" weapons and little concern for shareholders, a stark contrast with GE. Anders moved aggressively to correct this focus and instill an emphasis on shareholders and on metrics like return on equity.

He also believed that operations would need to be significantly streamlined to optimize returns. To accomplish this, he needed a new team, and he moved quickly to put one in place. His first step was to elevate Jim Mellor to president and chief operating officer. Mellor had run General Dynamics' shipbuilding business with excellent results, and as Anders told me, "He was the kind of guy that would look for the last nickel and hold people responsible." Together, in the first half of 1991, Anders and Mellor replaced twenty-one of the company's top twenty-five executives.

In addition to new operating talent, Anders brought on Harvey Kapnick, a financial wizard, as vice-chairman, and he began to rely on a talented lawyer, Nick Chabraja, to help with a variety of legal and strategic tasks relating to the turnaround. Once he had his team in place, he wasted little time in implementing an extraordinary restructuring.

. . .

The Anders years (only three in total) can be divided into two basic phases: the generating of cash and its deployment. In each phase, the company's approach was highly idiosyncratic.

Let's start with cash generation. When Anders and Mellor began to implement their plan, General Dynamics was overleveraged and had negative cash flow. Over the ensuing three years, the company would generate *$5 billion* of cash. There were two basic sources of this astonishing influx: a remarkable tightening of operations and the sale of businesses deemed noncore by Anders's strategic framework.

In operations, Anders and Mellor found a legacy of massive overinvestment in inventory, capital equipment, and research and development. Together, they moved quickly to wring the excesses out of the system. When they visited an F-16 factory, they looked around and counted huge numbers of expensive F-16 canopies (the clear glass covering for the cockpit) in a facility that made one plane a week—Mellor's new rule: a two-canopy maximum. They found duplicate pieces of expensive and underutilized machinery in adjacent tank plants—Mellor combined the facilities. More generally, they discovered that plant managers carried far too much inventory and hadn't been calculating return on investment in their requests for additional capital.

This changed quickly under Mellor's watch, and he and Anders moved decisively to create a culture that relentlessly emphasized returns. Specifically, as longtime executive Ray Lewis says, "Cash return on capital became the key metric within the company and was always on our minds."[3] This was a first for the entire industry, which had historically had a myopic focus on revenue growth and new product development.

Importantly, this new discipline affected the company's approach to bidding on government contracts. Prior to Anders's arrival, the company, like its peers, had bid aggressively on a wide variety of contracts. In contrast, Anders and Mellor insisted the company bid on projects only when returns were compelling and the probability of winning was high. As a result, the number of bids shrank dramatically, and the company's success rate rose. As longtime industry analyst Peter Aseritis says, "Anders and Mellor brought a new focus on shareholders . . . a first in the defense industry."[4]

In the first two years of their regime, Anders and Mellor reduced overall head count by nearly 60 percent (and corporate staff by 80 percent), relocated corporate headquarters from St. Louis to northern Virginia, instituted a formal capital approval process, and dramatically reduced investment in working capital. As Mellor said, "For the first couple of years we didn't need to spend *anything,* we could simply run off the prior years' buildup of inventories and capital expenditures."[5]

These moves produced a tsunami of cash—a remarkable *$2.5 billion*—and the company quickly became the unquestioned leader among its peers in return on assets, a position it holds to this day.

. . .

Which brings us to the other larger-than-expected source of cash at the company: asset sales. While Mellor was wringing excess cash from the operations, Anders set out to divest noncore businesses and grow his largest business units through acquisition. Interestingly, as Anders met with his industry peers, he found that, as a group, they were more interested in buying than selling. He also found that they were often willing to pay premium prices. The result was a dramatic shrinking of the company through a series of highly accretive divestitures.

This was a first for the company and for the industry. In the first two years, after taking the reins as CEO, Anders sold the *majority* of General Dynamics' businesses, including its IT division, the Cessna aircraft business, and the missiles and electronics businesses.

The largest of these divestitures, the sale of the company's dominant military aircraft business, presented an unexpected challenge to Anders's strategic framework and is worth looking at in more detail. This transaction actually began as an attempt by Anders to acquire Lockheed's smaller fighter plane division. When Lockheed's CEO refused to sell and made an extravagant counteroffer for General Dynamics' F-16 business, Anders faced a pivotal decision.

It's worth pausing here to make a more general point. Most of the CEOs in this book avoided detailed strategic plans, preferring to stay flexible and opportunistic. In contrast, Anders had a very clear and specific strategic vision that called not only for selling weaker divisions but for building up larger ones. After making early progress on the sales front, he turned his attention to acquisition, and the military aircraft unit, the company's largest business, was a logical place to start. On top of the economic logic of growing this sizable business unit, Anders, a former fighter pilot and an aviation buff, loved it. So when Lockheed's CEO surprised him by offering $1.5 billion, a mind-bogglingly high price for the division, Anders was faced with a moment of truth.

What he did is very revealing—he agreed to sell the business on the spot without hesitation (although not without some regret). Anders made the rational business decision, the one that was consistent with growing per share value, even though it shrank his company to less than half its former size and robbed him of his favorite perk as CEO: the opportunity to fly the company's cutting-edge jets. This single decision underscores a key point across the CEOs in this book: as a group, they were, at their core, rational and pragmatic, agnostic and clear-eyed. They did not have ideology. When offered the right price, Anders might not have sold his mother, but he didn't hesitate to sell his favorite business unit.

These sales were unprecedented in the industry and highly controversial, particularly within the Pentagon. Anders's distinguished military career, however, gave him unique credibility in Washington, which allowed him to pursue this radical course of action. As longtime defense analyst Peter Aseritis put it to me, "It was a little like Nixon, the longtime anticommunist, opening relations with China: no one else could have done it."[6] Collectively, these divestitures generated an additional $2.5 billion in cash and left General Dynamics with two businesses in which it held dominant market positions: tanks and submarines.

As the cash from asset sales and improved operations poured in, Anders shifted his focus to capital allocation. With prices high, he chose not to make additional acquisitions. Instead, he decided to return the majority of the company's cash to shareholders. For advice on how to do this in the most efficient manner, he turned to Harvey Kapnick.

Kapnick, the former chairman of accounting giant Arthur Andersen, was a lawyer by training and had deep knowledge of the tax code. He had made his reputation with an enormously successful turnaround at Chicago Pacific, a diversified conglomerate. As the cash built up at General Dynamics, he developed two creative ideas for returning the majority of it to shareholders in an extraordinarily tax-efficient manner.

First, Kapnick initiated a series of three special dividends to shareholders totaling just under 50 percent of the company's equity value. Because of the large percentage of General Dynamics' overall business that had been divested by Anders, these dividends were deemed "return of capital" and were, remarkably, subject to neither capital gains nor ordinary income taxes. As a next step, Anders and Kapnick announced a gigantic $1 billion tender to repurchase 30 percent of the company's shares (as we've seen, share repurchases are highly tax efficient versus traditional dividends, which are taxed at both the corporate and the individual levels).

It is hard to overstate how unusual these moves were: in less than three years, Anders had dramatically streamlined operations, sold off over half of his company, generated *$5 billion* in proceeds, and, rather than redeploying the cash into R&D or new acquisitions, returned most of it to shareholders, using innovative, tax-efficient techniques. Each of these moves was unprecedented in the defense industry and created enormous value for shareholders.

It is very, very rare to see a public company systematically shrink itself; as Anders summarized it to me, "Most CEOs grade

themselves on size and growth . . . very few really focus on shareholder returns." It is similarly rare (outside of the CEOs in this
book) to see a company systematically return proceeds to shareholders in the form of special dividends or share repurchases. The
combination of the two was virtually unheard of, particularly in
the tradition-bound defense industry.

. . .

This abrupt series of dramatic actions stunned Wall Street and
led to a meteoric rise in General Dynamics' stock price. It also
attracted Warren Buffett's attention. Buffett saw that under Anders's leadership, the company was divesting assets and focusing
on an innovative, shareholder-friendly capital allocation strategy,
and in 1992 he bought 16 percent of General Dynamics' stock at
an average price of $72 per share. Remarkably, he also gave An-
ders, whom he had only met once, the proxy to vote Berkshire's
shares, a position that aided Anders in implementing his strategy.

Anders left at the end of his planned term in July 1993, turning the reins over to Mellor (Buffett sold his shares on Anders's
departure for an excellent return, a decision, however, he regrets
today). Anders served as chairman for a year before retiring to a
remote island in the Northwest. He believed in the naval succession model in which retiring captains avoid returning to their
ships so as not to interfere with their successor's authority, and
proudly told me that he had spoken only once to Mellor's successor, Nick Chabraja, since 1997.

Jim Mellor had also trained as an engineer and worked at
Hughes Aircraft and Litton Industries before joining General
Dynamics in 1981. He eventually ran the shipbuilding division,

where he helped the company solidify its dominant market position and where he quickly came to Anders's attention as a kindred spirit and potential lieutenant and successor.

As CEO after Anders's departure, Mellor continued to focus on optimizing operations and selling the last small noncore divisions, including the space systems unit. In 1995, however, he went on the offensive with the $400 million acquisition of Bath Iron Works, one of the largest domestic builders of navy ships. This acquisition had enormous symbolic value, signaling to employees and the Pentagon that the company was now ready to grow again. As Mellor said, "The Bath acquisition put an end to rumors the company would be completely liquidated."[7] In 1997, Mellor hit retirement age and passed the baton to Nick Chabraja.

Chabraja had graduated from Northwestern law school and practiced corporate law for nearly twenty years with Jenner & Block, a top Chicago law firm. He worked with General Dynamics during the troubles of the 1980s, and by the time of Anders's arrival, had become a key adviser to the company. Anders quickly realized his potential, calling him "the most effective, business-like lawyer I've ever seen." In 1993, Chabraja joined the company as general counsel and senior vice president, with the implicit understanding that he would become Mellor's successor.

Chabraja set ambitious goals for himself when he became CEO. Specifically, he wanted to quadruple the company's stock price over his first ten years as CEO (a 15 percent compound rate of return). He looked back into S&P records and found that this was an appropriately difficult target: fewer than 5 percent of all *Fortune* 500 companies had achieved that benchmark in the prior ten-year period. Chabraja looked coolly at the company's prospects for the next ten years and concluded that he could get about two-thirds of the way there through market growth and improved operating margins. The rest would need to come from acquisitions, a notable departure from Anders's strategic framework.

Chabraja's approach to acquisitions was distinctive, focusing initially on small purchases around existing business lines, a new capital allocation focus for the company. As he said, "Our strategy has been to aggressively pursue targets directly related to our core businesses . . . broadening our product line into adjacent spaces."[8] In his first year, he bought twelve small companies.

Ray Lewis described this approach as "just a piece at a time in markets we understood well."[9] These add-on acquisitions were highly accretive and eventually led the company into the fast-growing military information technology market, which would become the company's largest business unit by 2008. Furthermore, through Chabraja's acquisition efforts, the company's tank division was able to successfully launch the Stryker attack vehicle, and the marine group, long a leader in submarine construction, began to build more surface ships.

The crowning achievement of the Chabraja era, however, was the massive 1999 acquisition of Gulfstream, the world's largest commercial jet manufacturer. This purchase was a $5 billion, bet-the-company transaction, equal to a remarkable 56 percent of General Dynamics' enterprise value.

The deal was widely criticized at the time for its seemingly high price and its apparent divergence from Anders's "focus only on defense businesses" strategy. It was not, however, as radical a departure as it appeared. Gulfstream was the unquestioned leader in commercial aviation, a market with excellent long-term growth trends. It had been run for five years by private equity firm Forstmann, Little, and investment in new product development had lagged.

General Dynamics had deep experience in managing both commercial and military aircraft operations from its years owning Cessna and building planes for the air force, and Chabraja believed he would be able to tap this latent expertise to grow Gulfstream significantly. He also believed that commercial aviation would provide valuable diversification against fluctuations in defense spending. The returns since that time have justified his logic. (Over the last couple of years as defense spending has slowed, Gulfstream's growing operations have provided General Dynamics with substantial insulation from the vagaries of the defense spending cycle.)

It's important to acknowledge here the more general point that circumstances vary, and it's how you play the hand you're dealt that ultimately determines your success as an executive. Although Chabraja and Anders shared a rational, shareholder-oriented mind-set, their specific actions varied with their respective circumstances, and different moves (acquisitions during Chabraja's tenure, divestitures during Anders's) made sense at different times during their tenures (although both shared an enthusiasm for stock repurchases).

By the time Chabraja stepped down as CEO in mid-2008, he had, remarkably, exceeded his initial ambitious return objectives. Which brings us to the key question: what exactly do the overall returns look like for this CEO troika? How do they stack up against their peers and the lofty Welch standard? Over the seventeen-and-a-half-year span, from Anders's arrival in January

1991 through Chabraja's departure in July 2008, Anders and his
two handpicked successors produced the phenomenal results that
can be seen in figure 3-1, generating a remarkable *23.3 percent*
compound annual return for General Dynamics' shareholders,
compared with *8.9 percent* for the S&P 500 and *17.6 percent* for
the company's peers.

**FIGURE 3-1**

## General Dynamics—a tale of three CEOs

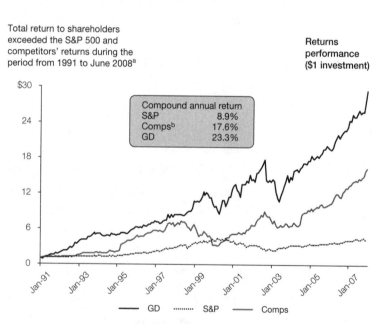

Total return to shareholders
exceeded the S&P 500 and
competitors' returns during the
period from 1991 to June 2008[a]

Returns
performance
($1 investment)

| Compound annual return | |
|---|---|
| S&P | 8.9% |
| Comps[b] | 17.6% |
| GD | 23.3% |

——— GD      ·········· S&P      ——— Comps

*Source:* Center for Research in Security Prices (CRSP) and General Dynamics annual reports.

a. Includes stock splits and stock dividends.
b. Comps include LMT (Lockheed Martin) and NOC (Northrop Grumman). Comps based on
weighted average of market value of equity as of January 1, 1991.

A dollar invested when Anders took the helm would have been worth *$30* seventeen years later. That same dollar would have been worth *$17* if invested in an index of peer companies and *$6* if invested in the S&P. This CEO triad exceeded the Welch standard with a *6.7 times* outperformance of the S&P and an exceptional *1.8 times* outperformance of its peers.

Today, General Dynamics looks very different than when Anders left the helm, yet his fundamental principles remain intact. General Dynamics is the unquestioned market leader in each of its business lines, with the industry's highest margins and return on assets and an impregnable balance sheet. In late 2007, Chabraja designated his successor, Jay Johnson. Johnson had an impressive résumé: he had been the youngest ever chief of naval operations and the CEO of electric utility giant Dominion Virginia Power prior to becoming vice-chairman at General Dynamics and heir designate. He has stepped, however, into very large shoes, and it will be up to him to maintain the company's extraordinary record in the uncertain years ahead.

Meanwhile, Bill Anders has settled into a typically active retirement on a remote island in the San Juans. He founded a well-regarded aviation museum outside Seattle and, well into his seventies, still flies jets. Although he has kept his distance from the company, he still holds the stock.

## The Nuts and Bolts

The key to these phenomenal returns was the company's highly effective (if unusual by defense industry standards) approach to allocating its human and capital resources. In the area of operations, Anders and his successors focused on two primary priorities: decentralizing the organization and aligning management compensation with shareholders' interests.

Not surprisingly, given the military background of many of its CEOs, the defense industry has traditionally been characterized by centralized, bureaucratic organizational structures. General Dynamics, however, under Anders and his two successors, pursued a very different organizational strategy. In the early 1990s, as they tightened operations and dramatically reduced headquarters staff, Anders and Mellor began to actively promote decentralization and push responsibility further down into the organization, eliminating layers of middle management. This move to decentralization would be continued and significantly extended by Chabraja.

By the end of Chabraja's tenure, the company would have more employees than when Anders arrived but only a quarter as many people at corporate headquarters. There would be only two people between the CEO and the head of any profit center, whereas before there had been four. All human relations, legal, and accounting personnel at headquarters were eliminated or pushed down into the operating divisions, and there was a conscious effort to keep staff involvement in the divisions to a minimum, to prevent headquarters from "screwing around with operating people," as Chabraja says. Operating managers were held responsible—in Chabraja's words, "severely accountable"—for hitting their budgets and were left alone if they did so.[10]

Starting with Anders, the company also began to emphasize performance-based compensation. In the early 1990s, Anders knew he would need to offer significant compensation upside to attract new managers to General Dynamics. He would have preferred to establish a traditional stock option program but was told by the board that shareholders, disgruntled by the stock's weak performance in the years prior to his arrival, would not approve one. Anders, however, wanted to align managers with shareholders, and developed a compensation plan that rewarded managers for sustained improvements in stock price.

The problem with this plan was that almost immediately after its implementation, the stock price moved quickly upward as Wall Street began to understand the effect of Anders's unusual moves, resulting in very early and large bonus payments to management. These payments were immediately seized on by the press and became highly controversial. The company, however, remained committed to performance-based compensation, and today bonus payments and option grants remain key components of executive pay at General Dynamics.

. . .

Under Anders and his successors, the company's approach to raising and allocating capital was highly differentiated from that of its defense industry peers. With the enormous proceeds from Anders's early divestitures and consistent, healthy operating cash flows, General Dynamics did not need to employ significant financial leverage or, with one very large exception, issue equity.

That exception, however, helps make an important point about capital allocation. The central event of Chabraja's tenure was the Gulfstream acquisition. So, how exactly did he pay for this massive deal? His approach was opportunistic and unusual—in a radical departure from the Anders playbook, Chabraja sold stock. A lot of stock. This was a seemingly dilutive move. Closer examination, however, reveals its sophistication (and kinship with Anders's principles).

As figure 3-2 shows, the equity offering coincided with an all-time high trading multiple for General Dynamics' stock (not unlike Buffett's large purchase of Gen Re, also done with a stock currency then trading at a record premium).

As Chabraja described it to me, "What drove me was the realization that the stock was trading at a significant premium to our historic norm: twenty-three times next year's projected earnings versus an historic average of sixteen times. So what do you do with a high-priced stock? Use it to acquire a premium asset in a related field at a lower multiple and benefit from the arbitrage."[11]

**FIGURE 3-2**

### P/E ratio—based on average P/E by year

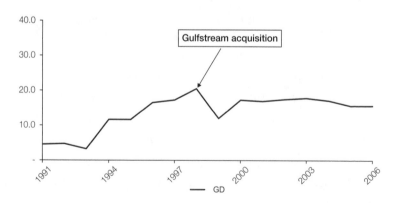

*Source:* Center for Research in Security Prices (CRSP) and General Dynamics annual report.

As Ray Lewis summarized, "Nick sold shares equaling one-third of the company to acquire a business that provided half of our consolidated operating cash flow."[12]

As with Anders's sale of the company's F-16 business, Chabraja's equity sale underscores the important point that the best capital allocators are practical, opportunistic, and flexible. They are not bound by ideology or strategy. In 1999, Chabraja saw a unique opportunity to grow and diversify his company by utilizing a uniquely inexpensive currency, and he grabbed it, adding significant economic value for his shareholders.

·  ·  ·

So, what exactly did this troika do with all the cash?

When it came to capital allocation, Anders and his successors made consistently, often radically, different decisions than their largest peers. At a time when his peers were on an acquisition binge, Anders, as we've seen, was an active *seller.* He made no acquisitions, spent very little on capital expenditures, and made savvy use of dividends and share repurchases, both of which were new to the industry.

After Anders's extended shrinking exercise, Mellor's major contribution in the allocation arena was to reopen the door to acquisitions with the sizable 1995 Bath transaction while continuing Anders's parsimonious approach to dividends and capital expenditures. Like Anders, Chabraja also pursued an idiosyncratic allocation strategy: spending meaningfully less money on capital expenditures and paying lower dividends than his peers while devoting substantial resources to acquisitions and sporadic stock repurchases.

The returns from these repurchases were excellent, averaging 17 percent over the entire period. All three CEOs were committed to buybacks, with Anders and Chabraja the most active in this important area. As we've seen, Anders's contribution in this area (with help from Kapnick) was the 1992 tender offer in which 30 percent of the company's shares were repurchased.

Interestingly, Chabraja was also an aggressive repurchaser of General Dynamics' stock. Belying his legal background, he thought like an investor, continually comparing the price of General Dynamics' stock with its intrinsic value and acting aggressively when he saw discrepancies. As Ray Lewis said of the Chabraja era, "We bought heavily when we thought we could take advantage of market mistakes in pricing our stock."[13]

. . .

Anders and Chabraja had similar, curmudgeonly personalities. Both were feistily iconoclastic, and neither suffered fools gladly (an attitude that was by no means atypical within the broader outsider CEO group). They handled themselves with Wall Street analysts in much the same manner that football coach Bill Parcells handles reporters, with an overall demeanor that often bordered on disdain. They simply did not see the value in courting analysts, and while Wall Street may not have entirely appreciated their prickliness, General Dynamics' shareholders certainly did.

## Postscript: The Sincerest Form of Flattery

If imitation is the sincerest form of flattery, then General Dynamics recently received a major compliment from Northrop

Grumman, one of the largest companies in the defense industry and a leading maker of fighter planes and missile systems. The company's stock market returns since the early 1990s have trailed General Dynamics' by a wide margin.

In 2009 a new CEO, Wes Bush, took over and announced a dramatic strategy shift that featured the sale of noncore assets, a new emphasis on return on equity and share repurchases, and a significant reduction in corporate head count. Sound familiar?

As one Wall Street analyst said, "The steps being taken at Northrop Grumman . . . are reminiscent of the changes taken by General Dynamics in the early 1990s . . . [and] are at odds with the typical behavior of defense companies, which have historically tended to overemphasize [revenue] growth . . . General Dynamics has dramatically outperformed other defense companies who continued to pursue scale . . . over the last 20 years."

Since Bush's announcement of this new strategy and the first signs of its implementation, Northrop's stock has risen dramatically. Today, in a very different foreign policy climate, the Anders formula remains every bit as effective and robust as it was when the Wall first came down.

## CHAPTER 4

# Value Creation in a Fast-Moving Stream

*John Malone and TCI*

They haven't repealed the laws of arithmetic . . . yet, anyway.

—*John Malone*

Luck is the residue of design.

—*Branch Rickey*

By 1970, John Malone had been at McKinsey long enough to know an attractive industry when he saw one, and the more Malone learned about the cable television business, the more he liked it. Three things in particular caught his attention: the highly predictable, utility-like revenues; the favorable tax characteristics; and the fact that it was growing like a weed. In his years at McKinsey, Malone had never before seen these characteristics in combination, and he quickly concluded that he wanted to build his career in cable.

The combination of high growth and predictability, in particular, was very attractive. During the 1960s and into the early 1970s, the cable industry exhibited very rapid growth, with subscriber counts growing over twentyfold, as rural communities across the country sought better reception of television signals for their favorite channels and programs. Cable television customers paid monthly and rarely disconnected, making the business highly quantifiable and allowing experienced executives to forecast customer growth and profitability with remarkable precision. This was a near-perfect fit with Malone's background, which was unusually quantitative. To paraphrase Norman Mailer, it was a case of Superman coming to Supermarket.

. . .

Malone was born in 1941 in Milford, Connecticut. His father was a research engineer and his mother a former teacher. Malone idolized his father, who traveled five days a week visiting plants for General Electric. As a teenager, he exhibited early mechanical ability and made pocket money buying, refurbishing, and selling used radios. He was athletic and competed in fencing, soccer, and track in high school. He graduated from Yale with a combined degree in economics and electrical engineering and almost immediately married his high school sweetheart, Leslie.

After Yale, Malone earned master's and PhD degrees in operations research at Johns Hopkins. His two academic fields, engineering and operations, were highly quantitative and shared a focus on optimization, on minimizing "noise" and maximizing "output." Indeed, Malone's entire future career can be thought of as an extended exercise in hyperefficient value engineering, in maximizing output in the form of shareholder value and minimizing noise from other sources, including taxes, overhead, and regulations.

After earning his PhD, Malone took a job at Bell Labs, the highly prestigious research arm of AT&T. There, he focused on studying optimal strategies in monopoly markets. After extensive financial modeling, he concluded that AT&T should increase its debt level and aggressively reduce its equity base through share repurchases. This unorthodox advice was graciously received by AT&T's board (and promptly ignored).

After a couple of years, Malone concluded that AT&T's bureaucratic culture was not for him, and he took a job with McKinsey Consulting. Having promised his wife that he would not duplicate his father's travel schedule, he soon found himself on the road four days a week working for a variety of *Fortune* 500 companies. In 1970, when one of those clients, General Instrument, offered him the opportunity to run Jerrold, its rapidly growing cable television equipment division, he leapt at the opportunity. He was twenty-nine years old.

At Jerrold, Malone actively cultivated relationships with the major cable companies, and after two years he was simultaneously courted by two of the largest operators: Steve Ross of Warner Communications and Bob Magness of Tele-Communications Inc. (TCI). Despite a salary that was 60 percent lower than Ross's offer, he chose TCI because Magness offered him a larger equity opportunity and because his wife preferred the relative calm of Denver to the frenetic pace of Manhattan.

The company Malone decided to join had a long history of aggressive growth and would soon be flirting with bankruptcy. Bob Magness had founded TCI in 1956, mortgaging his home to pay for his first cable system in Memphis, Texas. Magness, a peripatetic cottonseed salesman and rancher, had learned about the cable television business while hitchhiking, and like Malone fifteen years later, had immediately recognized its compelling economic characteristics. Magness was particularly quick to grasp the industry's favorable tax characteristics.

Prudent cable operators could successfully shelter their cash flow from taxes by using debt to build new systems and by aggressively depreciating the costs of construction. These substantial depreciation charges reduced taxable income as did the interest expense on the debt, with the result that well-run cable companies rarely showed net income, and as a result, rarely paid taxes, despite very healthy cash flows. If an operator then used debt to buy or build additional systems and depreciated the newly acquired assets, he could continue to shelter his cash flow indefinitely. Magness was among the first to fully recognize these attributes and made aggressive use of leverage to build his company, famously saying that it was "better to pay interest than taxes."

TCI went public in 1970 and, by 1973 when Malone joined, had become the fourth-largest cable company in the country, with six hundred thousand subscribers. Its debt at that time was equal to an astonishing seventeen times revenues. Magness had realized that he needed additional management talent to shepherd the company through the next phase of its growth, and after an extended courtship, had landed the McKinsey wunderkind. Malone brought an unusual combination of talents to TCI, including exceptional analytical ability, financial sophistication, technical savvy, and boldness. His tenure, however, got off to a rocky start.

In late 1972, the market for cable stocks was hot, and TCI planned an additional public offering to pay down a portion of its extraordinary debt load. Within months of Malone's arrival, however, the industry was blindsided by new regulations, and the market for cable stocks cooled, forcing the company to pull its offering and leaving it with an unsustainable debt position.

The sudden evaporation of liquidity that resulted from the 1973–1974 Arab oil embargo left the entire industry in a precarious position. TCI, however, with its new, thirty-two-year-old CEO, was burdened with significantly more debt than any of its peers and teetered on the edge of bankruptcy. "Lower than whale dung [sic]," is Malone's typically blunt assessment of his starting point at TCI.[1]

Malone had been dealt a tough hand, and he and Magness spent the next several years keeping the lenders at bay and the company out of bankruptcy. They met constantly with bankers. At one point in a particularly tense lender meeting, Malone threw his keys on the conference room table and walked out of the room, saying, "If you want the systems, they're yours." The panicked bankers eventually relented and agreed to amend the terms on TCI's loans.

During this period, Malone introduced a new financial and operating discipline to the company, telling his managers that if they could grow subscribers by 10 percent per year while maintaining margins, he would ensure that they stayed independent. A frugal, entrepreneurial culture emerged from these years and pervaded the company, extending from corporate headquarters down into field operations.

TCI's headquarters did not look like the headquarters of the largest company in an industry that was redefining the American media landscape. The company's offices were spartan, with few executives at corporate, fewer secretaries, and peeling metal desks on Formica floors. The company had a single receptionist, and an automated service answered the phone. TCI executives stayed together on the road, usually in motels—COO J. C. Sparkman recalls, "Holiday Inns were a rare luxury for us in those days."[2]

Malone saw himself as an investor and capital allocator, delegating responsibility for day-to-day operations to Sparkman, his longtime lieutenant, who managed the company's far-flung operations through a rigorous budgeting process. Managers were expected to hit their cash flow budget, and these targets were enforced with an almost military discipline by Sparkman, a for-

## The Edifice Complex

There is an apparent inverse correlation between the construction of elaborate new headquarters buildings and investor returns. As an example, over the last ten years, three media companies—The New York Times Company, IAC, and Time Warner—have all constructed elaborate, Taj Mahal–like headquarters towers in midtown Manhattan at great expense. Over that period, none of these companies has made significant share repurchases or had market-beating returns. In contrast, *not one* of the outsider CEOs built lavish headquarters.

mer air force officer. Managers in the field had a high degree of autonomy, as long as they hit their numbers. System managers who missed monthly budgets were frequently visited by the itinerant COO, and underperformers were quickly weeded out.

As a result of this frugality, TCI, for a long time, had the highest margins in the industry and gained a reputation with its investors and lenders as a company that consistently underpromised and overdelivered. In paging through analyst reports from early in the company's history, one can see a consistent recurring pattern of slightly higher-than-projected cash flow and subscriber numbers quarter after quarter.

. . .

By 1977, TCI had finally grown to the point that it was able to entice a consortium of insurance companies to replace the banks with lower-cost debt. With his balance sheet stabilized, Malone was finally able to go on the offensive and implement his strategy for TCI, which was highly unconventional and stemmed from a central strategic insight that had been germinating since he joined the company.

Malone, the engineer and optimizer, realized early on that the key to creating value in the cable television business was to maximize both financial leverage and leverage with suppliers, particularly programmers, and that the key to both kinds of leverage was size. This was a simple and deceptively powerful insight, and Malone pursued it with single-minded tenacity. As he told longtime TCI investor David Wargo in 1982, "*The* key to future profitability and success in the cable business will be the ability to control programming costs through the leverage of size."[3]

In a cable television system, the largest category of cost (40 percent of total operating expenses) is the fees paid to programmers (HBO, MTV, ESPN, etc.). Larger cable operators are able to negotiate lower programming costs per subscriber, and the more subscribers a cable company has, the lower its programming cost (and the higher its cash flow) per subscriber. These discounts continue to grow with size, providing powerful scale advantages for the largest players.

Thus, the largest player with the lowest programming costs would have a sustainable advantage in making new acquisitions versus smaller players—they would be able to pay more for a cable company and still earn the same or better returns, thereby creating a virtuous cycle of scale that went something like this: if you buy more systems, you lower your programming costs and increase your cash flow, which allows more financial leverage, which can then be used to buy more systems, which further improves your programming costs, and so on ad infinitum. The logic and power of this feedback loop now seems obvious, but no one else at the time pursued scale remotely as aggressively as Malone and TCI.

Related to this central idea was Malone's realization that maximizing earnings per share (EPS), the holy grail for most public companies at that time, was inconsistent with the pursuit of scale in the nascent cable television industry. To Malone, higher net income meant higher taxes, and he believed that the best strategy for a cable company was to use all available tools to *minimize* reported earnings and taxes, and fund internal growth and acquisitions with pretax cash flow.

It's hard to overstate the unconventionality of this approach. At the time, Wall Street evaluated companies on EPS. Period. For a long time, Malone was alone in this approach within the cable industry; other large cable companies initially ran their companies for EPS, only later switching over to a cash flow focus (Comcast finally switched in the mid-1980s) once they realized the difficulty of showing EPS while growing a cable business. As longtime cable analyst Dennis Leibowitz told me, "Ignoring EPS gave TCI an important early competitive advantage versus other public companies."[4]

While this strategy now seems obvious and was eventually copied by Malone's public peers, at the time, Wall Street did not know what to make of it. In lieu of EPS, Malone emphasized cash flow to lenders and investors, and in the process, invented a new vocabulary, one that today's managers and investors take for granted. Terms and concepts such as *EBITDA* (earnings before interest, taxes, depreciation, and amortization) were first introduced into the business lexicon by Malone. EBITDA in particular was a radically new concept, going further up the income statement than anyone had gone before to arrive at a pure definition of the cash-generating ability of a business before interest payments, taxes, and depreciation or amortization charges. Today EBITDA is used throughout the business world, particularly in the private equity and investment banking industries.

. . .

The market for cable stocks remained volatile throughout the 1970s and into the early 1980s. Malone and Magness, concerned about the potential for a hostile takeover, took advantage of occasional market downturns to opportunistically repurchase stock, thereby increasing their combined stake. In 1978, they created a supervoting class of B shares, and through a complex series of repurchases and trades, were able to secure what longtime executive John Sie refers to as "hard control" of TCI by 1979, when their combined ownership of B shares reached 56 percent.

From this point forward, with control and a healthier balance sheet, Malone focused on achieving scale with a unique combination of relentlessness and creativity. Using the debt available from the company's new lenders, internal cash flow, and the occasional equity offering, Malone began an extraordinarily active acquisition program. Between 1973 and 1989, the company closed 482 acquisitions, an average of one every other week. To Malone, a subscriber was a subscriber was a subscriber. As longtime investor Rick Reiss said, "In the pursuit of scale, he was willing to look at beachfront property even if it was near a toxic waste dump," and over the years, he bought systems from sellers as diverse as the Teamsters and Lady Bird Johnson.[5]

He did not, however, buy indiscriminately. In the late 1970s and early 1980s, the industry entered a new phase with the advent of satellite-delivered channels, such as HBO and MTV. Cable television suddenly went from a service primarily targeting rural customers with poor reception to one delivering highly desirable new channels to content-starved urban markets. As the industry entered this new stage, many of the larger cable companies began to focus on competing for large metropolitan franchises, and the bidding for these franchises quickly became heated and expensive.

Malone, however, unlike his peers, was uncomfortable with the extraordinary economic terms that municipalities were extracting from pliant cable operators, and alone among the larger cable companies, he refrained from these franchise wars, focusing instead on acquiring less expensive rural and suburban subscribers. By 1982, TCI was the largest company in the industry, with 2.5 million subscribers.

When many of the early urban franchises collapsed under a combination of too much debt and uneconomic terms, Malone stepped forward and acquired control at a fraction of the original cost. In this manner, the company gained control of the cable franchises for Pittsburgh, Chicago, Washington, St. Louis, and Buffalo.

Throughout the 1980s, aided by a very favorable mid-decade relaxation of FCC regulations, TCI continued to buy systems at an aggressive clip, mixing in occasional larger deals (Westinghouse and Storer Communications) with a steady stream of small transactions. In addition, the company continued to actively grow its portfolio of joint ventures, partnering with legendary cable entrepreneurs such as Bill Bresnan, Bob Rosenkranz, and Leo Hindery to create cable companies in which TCI owned minority stakes. By 1987, the company was twice the size of its next-largest competitor, Time Inc.'s ATC.

Malone's creativity further evidenced itself in a wave of joint ventures in the late 1970s and early 1980s in which he partnered with promising young programmers and cable entrepreneurs. A partial list of these partners reads like a cable hall of fame roster, including such names as Ted Turner, John Sie, John Hendricks, and Bob Johnson. In putting these partnerships together, Malone was in effect an extremely creative venture capitalist who actively sought young, talented entrepreneurs and provided them with access to TCI's scale advantages (its subscribers and programming discounts) in return for minority stakes in their businesses. In this way, he generated enormous returns for his shareholders. When he saw an entrepreneur or an idea that he liked, he was prepared to act quickly.

Beginning in 1979, when he famously wrote Bob Johnson, the founder of Black Entertainment Television (BET), a $500,000 check at the end of their first meeting, Malone began to actively pursue ownership stakes in programming entities, offering in re-turn a potent combination of start-up capital and access to TCI's millions of households. Malone led a consortium of cable com-panies in the bailout of Ted Turner's Turner Broadcasting Sys-tem (whose channels included CNN and The Cartoon Network) when it flirted with bankruptcy in 1987; and by the end of the 1980s, TCI's programming portfolio would include Discovery, Encore, QVC, and BET in addition to the Turner channels. He was now a significant owner of both cable systems and cable programming.

The early 1990s produced an almost perfect storm of bad news for the cable industry, with the combined impact of new highly leveraged transaction (HLT) legislation in 1990 limiting the in-dustry's access to debt capital and, more significantly, the FCC's tightening of cable regulations in 1993, which rolled back cable rates. Despite these negative developments, Malone continued to selectively acquire large cable systems (Viacom and United Artists Cable) and launch new programming networks, including Starz/

Encore and a series of regional sports networks in partnership with Rupert Murdoch and Fox.

In 1993, in a stunning development, Malone reached an agreement to sell TCI to phone giant Bell Atlantic for $34 billion in stock. The deal was called off, however, as reregulation hit and TCI's cash flow and stock price fell. As the decade progressed, Malone spent more time on projects outside of the core cable business. He led a consortium of cable companies in the creation of two sizable new entities: Teleport, a competitive telephone service, and Sprint/PCS, a joint venture with Sprint to bid on cellular franchises.

In pursuing these new initiatives, Malone was allocating the firm's capital and his own time to projects that he believed leveraged the company's dominant market position and offered compelling potential returns. In 1991, he spun off TCI's minority interests in programming assets into a new entity, Liberty Media, in which he ended up owning a significant personal stake. This was the first in a series of tracking stocks that Malone created, including TCI Ventures (for Teleport, Sprint/PCS, and other noncable assets) and TCI International (for TCI's ownership in miscellaneous foreign cable assets).

Malone was a pioneer in the use of spin-offs and tracking stocks, which he believed accomplished two important objectives: (1) increased transparency, allowing investors to value parts of the company that had previously been obscured by TCI's byzantine structure, and (2) increased separation between TCI's core cable business and other related interests (particularly programming) that might attract regulatory scrutiny. Malone started with the spin-off of the Western Tele-Communications micro-wave business in 1981, and by the time of the sale to AT&T, the company had spun off a remarkable fourteen different entities to shareholders. In utilizing these spin-offs, Malone, like Henry Singleton and Bill Stiritz, was consciously increasing the complexity of his business in pursuit of the best economic outcome for shareholders.

After Sparkman retired in 1995, Malone delegated authority for the company's cable operations to a new management team led by Brendan Clouston, a former marketing executive. Under Clouston, TCI began to centralize customer service and spend aggressively to upgrade its aging cable facilities. In the third quarter of 1996, however, TCI badly missed its forecast, losing subscribers for the first time in its history and showing a decline in quarterly cash flow. Malone, disappointed by these results, reassumed the helm and, uncharacteristically, took direct management control of operations, quickly reducing employee head count by twenty-five hundred, halting all orders for capital equipment, and aggressively renegotiating programming contracts. He also fired the consultants who had been hired to help with the system upgrade, and returned responsibility for customer service to the local system managers.

As operations stabilized and cash flow improved, he brought on Leo Hindery (the CEO of InterMedia Partners, a large TCI joint venture) to run operations, and returned his attention to strategic projects. Hindery continued the restructuring process: bringing back TCI veteran Marvin Jones as his COO, giving more responsibility to regional managers, and actively pursuing trades to more tightly cluster subscribers and reduce costs.

Once Hindery was on board, Malone focused his attention on developing digital set-top boxes that would allow the industry to compete effectively with the new satellite television providers. He courted Microsoft but eventually struck a deal with General Instrument, the industry's largest equipment manufacturer, for 10 million set-top boxes at $300 each. In return he asked for a significant equity stake in the company, eventually owning 16 percent.

In the middle of the operational crisis of 1996 and 1997, Bob Magness, Malone's mentor and longtime partner, died, throwing control of the company into question. Through a series of typically complex transactions, Malone was able, along with the company, to purchase Magness's supervoting shares, ensuring retention of "hard" control for the endgame phase at TCI.

. . .

In the late 1990s, several of Malone's strategic, noncable projects began to bear significant fruit. He had been correct about their return potential—in 1997, Teleport was sold to AT&T for an astounding $11 billion, a *twenty-eight-fold* return on investment. In 1998, the Sprint/PCS joint venture was sold to Sprint Corporation for $9 billion in Sprint stock, and in 1999, General Instrument was sold to Motorola for $11 billion.

In the late 1990s, Malone shifted his attention to finding a home for TCI. Although Malone loved the cable business, he was a purely rational executive and, as early as 1981, had told analyst David Wargo, "I felt TCI might be worth $48 a share and would sell if someone offered us this."[6] This target price continued to grow, and for a long, long time no one was willing to pay it. As the 1990s progressed, however, Malone saw a combination of factors clouding TCI's future: rising competition from satellite television, the enormous cost of upgrading the company's rural systems, and uncertainty about management succession. When he received an inquiry from AT&T's aggressive new CEO, Mike Armstrong, he eagerly initiated discussions. Characteristically, he handled the negotiations himself, often facing a sizable crowd of AT&T lawyers, bankers, and accountants across the table.

As talks between the two companies unfolded, Malone proved to be as adept at selling as he had been at acquiring. As Rick Reiss said, "He turned the board of AT&T upside down, shook every nickel from their pockets, and returned them to their board seats."[7] The financial terms—twelve times EBITDA, $2,600 per subscriber—were extraordinary and, remarkably, the company received no discount for its patchwork quilt of decrepit rural systems. Not surprisingly, Malone, ever watchful of unnecessary taxes, structured the transaction as a stock deal, allowing his investors to defer capital gains taxes.

In addition, Malone retained effective control of the Liberty programming subsidiary with six of nine board seats and secured an attractive, long-term carriage deal for Liberty's channels on AT&T's cable systems. This transaction was the final resounding validation of Malone's unique strategy at TCI: producing exceptional returns for his investors. Mind-boggling returns, in fact: in the twenty-five years after Malone took the helm at TCI, the entire cable industry grew enormously, and all the public companies in it prospered. No cable executive, however, created remotely as much value for shareholders as Malone. From his debut in 1973 until 1998 when the company was sold to AT&T, the compound return to TCI's shareholders was a phenomenal *30.3 percent,* compared with *20.4 percent* for other publicly traded cable companies and *14.3 percent* for the S&P 500 over the same period (see figure 4-1).

A dollar invested with TCI at the beginning of the Malone era was worth over *$900* by mid-1998. That same dollar was worth *$180* if invested in the other publicly traded cable companies and *$22* if invested in the S&P 500. Thus TCI outperformed the S&P by over *fortyfold* and its public peers by *fivefold* during Malone's tenure.

**FIGURE 4-1**

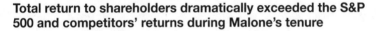

## Total return to shareholders dramatically exceeded the S&P 500 and competitors' returns during Malone's tenure

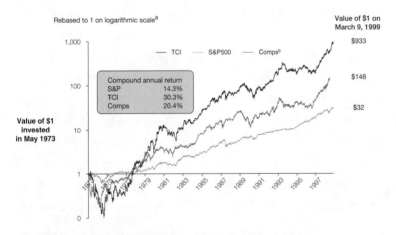

*Source:* Center for Research in Security Prices (CRSP) and TCI annual reports.

a. Includes stock splits and stock dividends.
b. Comps include Adelphia Communications, American Television & Communications, Cablevision Systems, Century Communications, Comcast, Cox Communications, Cox Cable, Falcon Cable Systems, Heritage Communications, Jones Intercable, Storer Broadcasting, TelePrompTer, and United Cable Television.

## The Nuts and Bolts

The cable television business during Malone's tenure was extremely capital intensive, with enormous amounts of cash required to build, buy, and maintain cable systems. As Malone sought to achieve scale by growing his subscriber base, three primary sources of capital were available to him in addition to TCI's robust operating cash flow: debt, equity, and asset sales. His use of each of these sources was distinctive.

Malone pioneered the active use of debt in the cable industry. He believed financial leverage had two important attributes: it magnified financial returns, and it helped shelter TCI's cash flow from taxes through the deductibility of interest payments. Malone targeted a ratio of five times debt to EBITDA and maintained it throughout most of the 1980s and 1990s. Scale allowed TCI to minimize its cost of debt, and Malone, having survived the harrowing experience of the mid-1970s, structured his debt with great care to lower costs and avoid cross-collateralization so that if one system defaulted on its debt, it would not affect the credit of the entire company. This compartmentalization into "bulkheads" (the term derived from Malone's fascination with all things nautical—he also sometimes referred to TCI's "bow wave of depreciation") caused further complexity in TCI's structure, but provided the company with substantial downside protection.

When it came to issuing equity, Malone was parsimonious, with the company's occasional offerings timed to coincide with record high multiples on his stock. As Malone said in a 1980 interview, "Our recent rise in stock price provided us with a good opportunity for this offering."[8] He was justifiably proud of his stinginess in issuing equity and believed it was another factor that distinguished him from his peers.

Malone occasionally and opportunistically sold assets. He coolly evaluated the public and private values for cable systems and traded actively in both markets when he saw discrepancies. Malone carefully managed the company's supply of net operating losses (NOLs), accumulated over years of depreciation and interest deductions, which allowed him to sell assets without paying taxes. As a result of this tax shield, he was comfortable selling systems if prices were attractive, to raise capital to fund future growth. As Malone told David Wargo as early as 1981, "It makes sense to maybe sell off some of our systems . . . at 10 times cash flow to buy back our stock at 7 times."[9]

Another key source of capital at the company was taxes not paid. As we've seen, tax minimization was a central component of Malone's strategy at TCI, and he took Magness's historical approach to taxes to an entirely new level. Malone abhorred taxes; they offended his libertarian sensibilities, and he applied his engineering mind-set to the problem of minimizing the "leakage" from taxes as he might have minimized signal leakage on an electrical engineering exam. As the company grew its cash flow by twentyfold over Malone's tenure, it never paid significant taxes.

In fact, Malone's one extravagance in terms of corporate staff was in-house tax experts. The internal tax team met *monthly* to determine optimal tax strategies, with meetings chaired by Malone himself. When he sold assets, he almost always sold for stock (the reason that, to this day, Liberty has large holdings of News Corp., Time Warner, Sprint, and Motorola stock) or sheltered gains through accumulated NOLs, and he made constant use of the latest tax strategies. As Dennis Leibowitz said, "TCI hardly ever disposed of an asset unless there was a tax angle to it."[10] No other cable company devoted remotely as much time and attention to this area as TCI.

. . .

Given the extraordinary growth in cable during the 1970s and 1980s, Malone had the luxury of high-return capital allocation options, and he structured TCI to optimize across them. As one might expect from his background, Malone had a coolly rational, almost surgical approach to capital allocation, and he was willing to look at any investment project that offered attractive returns regardless of complexity or unconventionality. Applying his engineering mind-set, Malone looked for no-brainers, focusing only on projects that had compelling returns. Interestingly, he didn't use spreadsheets, preferring instead projects where returns could be justified by simple math. As he once said, "Computers require an immense amount of detail . . . I'm a mathematician, not a programmer. I may be accurate, but I'm not precise."

In deciding how to deploy TCI's capital, Malone made choices that were starkly different from those of his peers. He never paid dividends (or even considered them) and rarely paid down debt. He was parsimonious with capital expenditures, aggressive in regard to acquisitions, and opportunistic with stock repurchases.

Until the advent of satellite competition in the mid-1990s, Malone saw no quantifiable benefit to improving his cable infrastructure unless it resulted in new revenues. To him, the math was undeniably clear: if capital expenditures were lower, cash flow would be higher. As a result, for years Malone steadfastly re-fused to upgrade his rural systems despite pleas from Wall Street. As he once said in a typically candid aside, "These [rural systems] are our dregs and we will not attempt to rebuild them."[11] This attitude was very different from that of the leaders of other cable companies who regularly trumpeted their extensive investments in new technologies.

Ironically, this most technically savvy of cable CEOs was typi-cally the last to implement new technology, preferring the role of technological "settler" to that of "pioneer." Malone appreciated how difficult and expensive it was to implement new technolo-gies, and preferred to wait and let his peers prove the economic viability of new services, saying of an early-1980s decision to delay the introduction of a new setup box, "We lost no major ground by waiting to invest. Unfortunately, pioneers in cable technology often have arrows in their backs." TCI was the last public company to introduce pay-per-view programming (and when it did, Malone convinced the programmers to help pay for the equipment).

He was, however, prepared to invest when he needed to, and he was among the first in the industry to champion expensive new set-top boxes to help increase channel capacity and customer choice when satellite competition arose in the mid-1990s.

Far and away the largest capital allocation outlet for TCI was, of course, acquisitions. As we've seen, Malone was an aggressive, yet disciplined, buyer of cable systems, a seeming oxymoron. He bought more companies than anybody else—in fact, he bought more companies than his three or four largest competitors com-bined. Collectively, these acquisitions represented an enormous bet on the future of cable, an industry long characterized by regulatory uncertainty and potential competitive threats; and from 1979 through 1998, the average *annual* value of TCI's acquisitions equaled a remarkable 17 percent of enterprise value (exceeding 20 percent in five of those years).

He was also, however, a value buyer, and he quickly developed a simple rule that became the cornerstone of the company's acquisition program: only purchase companies if the price translated into a maximum multiple of five times cash flow after the easily quantifiable benefits from programming discounts and overhead elimination had been realized. This analysis could be done on a single sheet of paper (or if necessary, the back of a napkin). It did not require extensive modeling or projections.

What mattered was the quality of the assumptions and the ability to achieve the expected synergies, and Malone and Sparkman trained their operations teams to be highly efficient in eliminating unnecessary costs from new acquisitions. Immediately after TCI took over the floundering Pittsburgh franchise from Warner Communications, it reduced payroll by half, closed the elaborate studios the prior owners had built for the city, and moved headquarters from a downtown skyscraper to a tire warehouse. Within months, the formerly unprofitable system was generating significant cash flow.

Malone's simple rule allowed him to act quickly when opportunity presented itself. When the Hoak family, owners of a million-subscriber cable business, decided to sell in 1987, Malone was able to strike a deal with them in an hour. He was also comfortable walking away from transactions that did not meet the rule. Paul Kagan, a longtime industry analyst, remembered

Malone walking away from a sizable Hawaiian transaction that was only $1 million over his target price.

Malone, alone among the CEOs of major public cable companies, was also an opportunistic buyer of his own stock during periodic market downturns. As Dennis Leibowitz said, "None of the other public MSO's [multiple system operators] made any significant share repurchases over this period."[12] In contrast, TCI repurchased over 40 percent of its shares during Malone's tenure. His timing with these purchases was excellent, producing an average compound return of over 40 percent.

An exchange with Dave Wargo in the early 1980s was typical of Malone's opportunistic philosophy regarding buybacks: "We are evaluating all alternatives in order to buy our equity at current prices to arbitrage the differential between its current multiple and the private market value."[13] These buybacks provided a useful benchmark in evaluating other capital allocation options, including acquisitions. As Malone said to Wargo in 1981, "With our stock in the low twenties . . . purchasing it looks more attractive than buying private systems."[14]

. . .

To the standard menu of five capital allocation alternatives, Malone added a sixth: investment in joint ventures. No CEO has ever used joint ventures as actively, or created as much value for his shareholders through them, as John Malone. Malone realized early on that he could leverage the company's scale into equity interests in programmers and other cable companies, and that these interests could add significant value for shareholders, with very little incremental investment. At the time of the sale to

AT&T, the company had *forty-one* separate partnership interests, and much of TCI's long-term return is attributable to these cable and noncable joint ventures.

Because of these polyglot joint ventures, TCI was notoriously hard to analyze and often sold at a discount to its cable peers. (As David Wargo said, "To understand the company you had to read *all* of their footnotes and very few did."[15]) Malone, however, believed this complexity was a small price to pay for the enormous value created over the years by these projects. As with many of Malone's initiatives, these joint ventures seem logical in hindsight, but at the time they were highly unconventional: no one else in the industry used joint ventures to increase system ownership, and only later did other MSOs begin to seek ownership stakes in programmers.

. . .

Despite his cool, calculating, almost Spock-like approach, Malone was also successful in creating a very strong culture and engendering great employee loyalty. He did this by providing a powerful mix of incentive and autonomy. TCI had an aggressive employee stock purchase program in which the company matched employee contributions and invited participation from all levels in the organization. Many early employees (supposedly including Malone's longtime secretary) became millionaires, and this culture bred tremendous loyalty—in Malone's first sixteen years at the helm, not a single senior executive left the company.

TCI's operations were remarkably decentralized, and as late as 1995, when Sparkman retired, the company had only seventeen employees at corporate in a company with 12 million subscribers. As Malone put it with characteristic directness, "We don't believe in staff. Staff are people who second-guess people." The company did not have human resource executives and didn't hire a PR person until the late 1980s. TCI's culture was described by Dennis Leibowitz as a group of frugal, action-oriented "cowboys" who defined themselves in counterpoint to the more conservative and bureaucratic Easterners who ran the other large cable companies.

. . .

Malone created a model for savvy capital allocation in rapidly growing, capital-intensive businesses that has been followed by executives in industries as diverse as cellular telephony, records management, and communications towers. Among the CEOs in this book, he most resembles that other high-level mathematician (and PhD), Henry Singleton. For mathematicians, insights often come when variables are taken to extremes, and Malone was no exception. Nothing about TCI was characterized by half measures. TCI was the largest company in the cable industry, with the lowest programming costs, least maintained facilities, most complex structure, and, oh yes, far and away the highest returns.

His management of TCI had a quality of asceticism about it. *Every* element of the company's strategy—from the pursuit of scale to tax minimization to the active use of financial leverage—was designed to optimize shareholder returns. As Malone said in summing up his analytically driven approach to building TCI, "They haven't repealed the laws of arithmetic . . . yet anyway." A fact for which his shareholders are eternally grateful.

# 5

# The Widow Takes the Helm

## *Katharine Graham and The Washington Post Company*

Establishing and maintaining an unconventional [approach] requires . . . frequently appearing downright imprudent in the eyes of conventional wisdom.

—*David Swensen, Chief Investment Officer, Yale University Endowment*

Katharine Graham's path to becoming chairman and CEO of The Washington Post Company was highly unusual. The daughter of prominent financier (and *Washington Post* owner) Eugene Meyer, she grew up in a privileged milieu of servants, boarding schools, country houses, and international travel. In 1940, she married Philip Graham, a brilliant Harvard-trained lawyer and protégé of Supreme Court justice Felix Frankfurter. Graham was tapped by Meyer in 1946 to run the company, which he would do with intermittent brilliance until his sudden death by suicide in 1963. After his tragic death, Katharine found herself thrust unexpectedly into the CEO role.

It is impossible to overstate Graham's unpreparedness for this position. At age forty-six, she was the mother of four and hadn't been regularly employed since the birth of her first child nearly twenty years before. With Phil's unexpected death, she suddenly found herself the only female chief executive of a *Fortune* 500–size company. Naturally shy, she was understandably terrified. This story, although remarkable, is well known (the best version by far being Graham's own Pulitzer Prize–winning autobiography, *Personal History,* published in 1997).

What's less well appreciated is what Graham did for her shareholders. From the time of the company's IPO in 1971 until she stepped down as chairman in 1993, the compound annual return to shareholders was a remarkable *22.3 percent,* dwarfing both the S&P (*7.4 percent*) and her peers (*12.4 percent*). A dollar invested at the IPO was worth *$89* by the time she retired, versus *$5* for the S&P and *$14* for her peer group. As figure 5-1 shows, she outperformed the S&P by *eighteenfold* and her peers by over *sixfold.* She was simply the best newspaper executive in the country during this twenty-two-year period by a very wide margin.

. . .

When Graham assumed the presidency of The Washington Post Company on September 20, 1963 (only two months before the death of her friend John F. Kennedy), she inherited a company

FIGURE 5-1

## The Washington Post Company's (WPO) total return to shareholders dramatically exceeded the S&P 500 and competitors' returns during Graham's tenure[a]

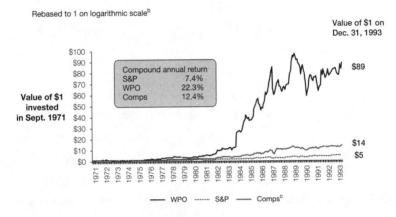

Source: Center for Research in Security Prices

a. For purposes of this figure, Graham's tenure is assumed to begin in 1971 (rather than 1963) when WPO went public.
b. Includes stock splits and stock dividends.
c. Comps include Gannett Co., Knight Ridder, Media General, The New York Times Company, and Times Mirror Company, weighted by market cap.

that had grown significantly under Phil's leadership and owned a portfolio of media assets, including the *Post* itself (one of three papers in the growing DC market), *Newsweek* magazine, and three television stations in Florida and Texas.

For the next few years, she took her time settling into her new position and familiarizing herself with the business and her board and management team. Starting in 1967, she began to make her presence felt when she made her first significant personnel decision, replacing longtime *Post* editor in chief Russ Wiggins with the brash, forty-four-year-old Ben Bradlee, a relatively unproven assistant editor at *Newsweek*.

In 1971, on the advice of her board, she filed to take the company public in order to raise capital for acquisitions. Within a week of the offering, the newspaper became embroiled in the Pentagon Papers crisis, which presented an opportunity to publish a highly controversial (and negative) internal Pentagon assessment of the war in Vietnam that a court had barred the *New York Times* from publishing. The Nixon administration, fearing a fresh wave of negative publicity on the war, threatened to challenge the company's broadcast licenses if it published the report. Such a challenge would have scuttled the stock offering and threatened one of the company's primary profit centers. Graham, faced with unclear legal advice, had to make the decision entirely on her own. She decided to go ahead and print the story, and the *Post*'s editorial reputation was made. The Nixon administration did not challenge the TV licenses, and the offering, which raised $16 million, was a success.

In 1972, the *Washington Post,* with Graham's full support, began intensive investigations into the Republican campaign improprieties that would eventually mushroom into the Watergate imbroglio. Bradlee and two young investigative reporters, Carl Bernstein and Bob Woodward, would spearhead the coverage of this extraordinary scandal, which would eventually lead to Richard Nixon's resignation in the summer of 1974. This journalistic coup secured a Pulitzer for the *Post* (one of a remarkable eighteen during Bradlee's editorship) and established it as the only journalistic peer to the *New York Times*. The rumblings and threats from the Nixon administration continued throughout Watergate, and Graham resolutely ignored them.

Graham used a portion of the proceeds from the public offering to buy the New Jersey–based *Trenton Times,* which proved to be a mediocre acquisition. The *Times* was an afternoon paper in a competitive two-paper market, and it struggled to grow. Graham learned a valuable lesson from this experience and would be appropriately cautious about acquisitions going forward.

In 1974, a new and unknown investor began to accumulate stock in the company, eventually buying 13 percent of its shares. Ignoring the advice of her board, Graham met with the newcomer, Warren Buffett, and invited him to join the board. Buffett would quickly become her business mentor and would help her navigate an unorthodox course for the company.

In 1975, the company faced a massive strike led by the powerful pressmen's union, which began when strikers set fire to the printing facility. Graham, after consulting with Buffett and the rest of her board, decided to fight the strike. After missing only one day of publication, she and Bradlee (and her twenty-seven-year-old son, Donald) assembled a skeleton crew that managed to get the paper out for 139 consecutive days until the pressmen finally agreed to accept significant concessions.

This strike was a harrowing experience for all involved (at one point one of the picketers was spotted wearing a shirt that read, "Phil shot the wrong Graham"), but these concessions dramatically improved the *Post*'s profitability and represented a turning point for the entire industry—one of the first times a major metropolitan paper had ever broken a strike. For Graham, the strike was a personal turning point, the business equivalent of Water-gate. From this point forward, there was no question who was in charge at The Washington Post Company.

. . .

It was at this time, coached by Buffett, that Graham made another unconventional decision and began aggressively buying her own stock, something very few people (outside of Henry Singleton and Tom Murphy) were even thinking about at the time. Over the next several years, she would repurchase almost 40 percent of the company's shares at rock-bottom prices. Significantly, none of her peers at other major newspaper companies followed her lead.

In 1981, two significant events occurred. First, the *Post's* long-time rival, the *Washington Star,* after years of declining circulation, finally ceased publication. This left the *Post,* with its lean, poststrike cost structure, as the monopoly daily newspaper in the nation's capital, which led to a dramatic increase in circulation and profitability that continued throughout the decade.

The second development was even more significant. After four previous attempts during the decade of the 1970s, Graham finally found a strong chief operating officer in Dick Simmons. Simmons, who had been the COO at Dun & Bradstreet, another diversified media company, wasted little time in rationalizing the company's operating units, which were running at lower margins than peer companies. His arrival ushered in an era of greatly increased profitability and further underscores the critical role played by strong operating lieutenants in the success of the outsider CEOs.

Simmons, with Graham's support, brought in new executive talent, divested the Trenton paper, changed the compensation structure to emphasize bonus compensation, and insisted on strong performance relative to peers. Within several years, the company's newspaper and television margins had almost doubled, resulting in a surge in profitability.

The 1980s represented a new high-water mark for deal making in the newspaper industry. Prices skyrocketed as both profits and multiples rose precipitously. Alone among major newspaper company executives, Graham stood on the sidelines. The company looked closely at many deals, including large papers in Iowa, Texas, and Kentucky, but it made only two acquisitions, both of them small. It's important to recognize how unusual this restrained behavior was in the hothouse climate of the mid- to late 1980s. It was a lonely path that elicited much commentary from Graham's peers and the press, a particularly difficult position for the only female executive in a high-profile, clubby, male-dominated industry.

Importantly, most of the Post Company's acquisitions under Graham would lead it into new businesses, unrelated to newspapers or broadcasting. In 1983, after extensive research by one of Simmons's new hires, a former management consultant named Alan Spoon, the company made a successful foray into the cellular telephone business, buying franchises in six metropolitan markets, including Detroit, Washington, and Miami, for $29 million. In 1984, she acquired the Stanley Kaplan test preparation business, establishing a toehold in the education market. Finally, in 1986, Graham, thanks to a timely introduction by Buffett, made her largest acquisition ever: the purchase of Capital Cities' cable television assets for $350 million. Each of these businesses would prove enormously important for the Post Company in the years ahead.

In early 1988, as values skyrocketed and Graham began to appreciate the large capital expenditures required to develop its cellular systems, she made a rare divestiture, deciding to sell the company's telephone assets for $197 million, an extraordinary return on its investment.

During the recession of the early 1990s, when her overleveraged peers were forced to the sidelines, the company became uncharacteristically acquisitive, taking advantage of dramatically lower prices to opportunistically purchase cable television systems, underperforming TV stations, and a few education businesses.

When Kay Graham stepped down as chairman in 1993, the Post Company was by far the most diversified among its newspaper peers, earning almost half its revenues and profits from nonprint sources. This diversification would position the company for further outperformance under her son Donald's leadership.

Graham did an excellent job of managing her succession (not a given at family-controlled firms) and spent the late 1980s and early 1990s readying the next generation of leaders at the company, including Donald, who would replace her as CEO in 1991; and Alan Spoon, who would replace his mentor, Dick Simmons, as COO, also in 1991. As Graham stepped down at age seventy-six, talented, younger managers would also assume leadership roles at the company's increasingly important cable (Tom Might) and education (Jonathan Grayer) divisions. Their talent and leadership would position the Post Company for another fifteen years of outperformance versus its peers.

## The Nuts and Bolts

Graham, under Buffett's tutelage, proved to be a highly effective, if unorthodox, capital allocator. Her approach in this important area was characterized by industry-low levels of dividends and debt, an industry-high level of stock repurchases, relatively few acquisitions, and a careful approach to capital expenditures. We'll look now at these areas, starting with the company's sources of capital.

During Graham's tenure, the Post Company generated consistently strong cash flow, with profitability improving dramatically during the decade of the 1980s as newspaper revenue spiked after the *Star* folded, and Dick Simmons increased margins across all the operating units. In addition to this wave of cash, the company had two other sources of capital, both of them rarely employed: leverage and asset sales.

Graham was generally reticent about using debt, and during her tenure, the Post consistently maintained the most conservative balance sheet among its peers. Graham raised significant debt only a few times during her tenure, most notably to finance the 1986 purchase of the Capital Cities cable systems. The Post's strong cash flow, however, allowed the bulk of this debt load to be paid down in less than three years.

Under Graham, the Post Company, like Buffett's Berkshire, very rarely sold operating businesses and actively eschewed spin-offs, preferring instead the long-term direct ownership model. The company made its lone significant exception in early 1988 when it decided to sell its cellular assets, generating an extraordinary return on investment.

. . .

Graham deployed this cash with great care. Throughout her tenure, she maintained a minimal level of dividends, believing them to be tax inefficient. Again, it's worth emphasizing the contrarian nature of this approach particularly in the newspaper industry, where founding families, some of whose members typically depended on the dividend income, usually had a high degree of ownership. The Post, under Graham, consistently paid the lowest level of dividends among its peer group and thus had the highest retained earnings.

Graham's approach to deploying these earnings was influenced by Simmons, Buffett, and another director, Dan Burke of Capital Cities. All capital expenditure decisions were submitted to a rigorous approval process, which required attractive returns on invested capital. As Alan Spoon summarized it, "The system was totally federalized, with all excess cash sent to corporate. Managers had to make the case for all capital projects. The key question was, 'Where's the next dollar best applied?' And the company was rigorous and skeptical in answering that question."[1]

This discipline led Graham to a more cautious approach to physical plant investments than that of her peers. During the 1980s, other large newspaper companies spent hundreds of millions of dollars to install new printing and prepress facilities that allowed shorter lead times and color printing. Graham, alone among major newspaper CEOs, held back, eventually becoming the last major publisher to rely on old-fashioned letterpress printing, deferring the expensive investment in a new plant until costs had dropped and the benefits had been definitively proven out by peers.

Graham's approach to acquisitions was characterized by the twin themes of patience and diversification. Graham's years at the helm from the IPO on were characterized by generally rising earnings and multiples for media companies punctuated by two severe bear markets, one in the mid-1970s and one in the early 1990s. In other words, the *value* of media properties fluctuated wildly over her tenure, and she proved herself to be an astute navigator of these trends.

Graham's activity level was a mirror image of this macroeconomic picture, with two significant periods of stock repurchase and acquisition at the beginning and the end of her career, bookending a long period of inactivity that accounted for the vast majority of her tenure.

With her board, she subjected all potential transactions to a rigorous, analytical test. As Tom Might summarized it, "Acquisitions needed to earn a minimum 11 percent cash return without leverage over a ten-year holding period." Again, this seemingly simple test proved a very effective filter, and as Might says, "Very few deals passed through this screen. The company's whole acquisition ethos was to wait for just the right deal."[2]

As we've seen, during the acquisition frenzy of the 1980s, Graham generally stood aside, passing on numerous newspaper acquisitions, large and small. As her son Donald says today, "The deals not done were very important. Another large newspaper would have been a boat anchor around our necks today."[3] The only newspaper investment that the company made during the decade was telling—the purchase of a minority interest in Cowles Media, the publisher of the *Minneapolis Star Tribune* and several smaller dailies. The interest was purchased outside of an auction at an attractive price, based on a long relationship between the Graham and Cowles families.

Buffett played a key role in this discipline, functioning as Graham's allocation court of appeals and weighing in on all significant decisions involving capital investment. He was particularly involved with acquisitions. Buffett's style, however, was not directive, according to longtime board member and Cravath, Swaine partner George Gillespie: "He would never say, 'Don't do that,' but something more subtle, along the lines of, 'I probably wouldn't do that for these reasons, but I'll support whatever you decide.'"[4] His reasoning, however, was invariably compelling and usually encouraged restraint.

Most of the Post's acquisitions under Graham would lead the company into new businesses, unrelated to newspapers or broadcasting, where competition was less intense and valuations more reasonable. The most significant of these diversifying purchases were the Stanley Kaplan test preparation business, which provided a toehold in the education market, and the large 1986 Capital Cities acquisition, which established an entry point into the rapidly growing cable business.

The Capital Cities cable deal was both very large and highly opportunistic, and, like the Cowles deal, revealing of Graham's disciplined approach to acquisitions. When Capital Cities was forced by the FCC to divest its cable television systems following the ABC acquisition, Warren Buffett arranged for the *Post* to get an exclusive look at the transaction. Graham sensed a potentially compelling, proprietary opportunity. After a frenzied weekend, she and her team agreed to acquire the systems for an attractive price of $1,000 per subscriber. Importantly, no investment banker was involved.

. . .

Graham's uncharacteristic buying spree during the recession of the early 1990s was also telling. With an exceptionally strong balance sheet, she became an active buyer at a time when her over-leveraged peers were forced to the sidelines. Taking advantage of dramatically reduced prices, the Post opportunistically purchased a series of rural cable systems, several underperforming television stations in Texas, and a number of education businesses, all of which proved to be extremely accretive to shareholders.

As we've seen, stock repurchases were another major capital allocation outlet for Graham. Once Buffett explained the compelling math of repurchases, she initiated a buyback program and pursued it with vigor. Graham would add enormous value for her shareholders by buying in a massive amount of stock (almost 40 percent eventually), most of it purchased during the 1970s and early 1980s at single-digit P/E multiples. As longtime investor Ross Glotzbach of Southeastern Asset Management says, "All buybacks are not created equal—she purchased in big chunks and at the right time."[5] As figure 5-2 shows, she was alone among newspaper executives in aggressively repurchasing shares and had to overcome strong initial resistance from her board. As George Gillespie says, "In those days, buying back stock was *very* unusual."[6] (Buffett, who originally owned 13 percent of the company, never sold a share and today owns over 22 percent.)

FIGURE 5-2

## WPO was the only member of its peer group to repurchase a significant percentage of its outstanding shares (38.5 percent)

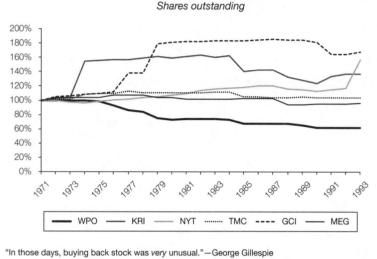

*Shares outstanding*

"In those days, buying back stock was *very* unusual." —George Gillespie

*Source:* Compustat and Center for Research in Security Prices (CRSP).

Ironically, in the early 1980s, the management consulting firm McKinsey advised the company to halt its buyback program. Graham followed McKinsey's advice for a little over two years, before, with Buffett's help, coming to her senses and resuming the repurchase program in 1984. Donald Graham reckons this high-priced McKinsey wisdom cost Post shareholders hundreds of millions of dollars of value, calling it the "most expensive consulting assignment ever!"

·  ·  ·

On the broader topic of resource allocation, one of Graham's defining managerial traits was a unique ability to identify and attract talent to her company and her board. Although she could seem aloof, she had terrific people instincts, and as Alan Spoon told me, "She was a consummate 'convener.'"[7] While some of these people were paragons of the establishment—including directors such as former defense secretary Robert McNamara, and a succession of lawyers from the white-shoe firm of Cravath, Swaine in New York—many of her choices were decidedly unconventional. Two in particular stand out.

First, in 1967, as we've seen, she tapped Ben Bradlee, a young and relatively unknown *Newsweek* assistant managing editor, to replace longtime *Post* editor in chief Russ Wiggins. It's hard to overstate the unconventionality of this decision. Probably the most important personnel decision the head of a newspaper company makes is the choice of an editor in chief, the person with overall responsibility for the content and voice of the paper. Graham had concluded that she needed a younger editor, one more attuned to the rapidly changing political landscape and culture of the late 1960s. When she first mentioned the idea to the salty Bradlee over lunch, he famously responded, "I'd give my left one for that job." Bradlee, who had no prior newspaper management experience, could not have been more different from the distinguished, professorial Wiggins.

He would, however, prove to be a bold and intuitive editor who would lead the paper through the glory and turmoil of its 1970s scoops. He was also a magnet for attracting top young journalistic talent to the paper. This influx of talent, along with innovations such as the introduction of the country's first style section, led to consistent circulation gains through the 1970s and into the 1980s, providing a critical engine of profit growth for the company.

Her second decision occurred during the severe bear market of 1974, when a new investor accumulated a large chunk of the Post's stock, causing ripples of anxiety at the company. The board in particular was suspicious of this newcomer and his intentions. Graham had inherited a board composed of experienced local businessmen and cronies of her husband's. Although increasingly assertive in journalistic matters, she still frequently deferred to their judgment and advice on business matters.

In this case, however, she struck out on her own and decided to meet with the new investor. To her credit, she immediately recognized his unique abilities, and against her board's advice, she invited the newcomer onto the board and moved to secure him as her key business confidant and adviser, instructing him only to "be gentle and not hurt my feelings."[8]

The decision to welcome Buffett into the fold was a highly independent and unusual one at the time. In the mid-1970s, Buffett was virtually unknown. Again, the choice of a mentor is a critically important decision for any executive, and Graham chose unconventionally and extraordinarily well. As her son Donald has said, "Figuring out this relatively unknown guy was a genius was one of the less celebrated, best moves she ever made."

A third personnel decision—more conventional, but no less important—involved the hiring of Simmons in 1981. Given her inexperience with operations, the chief operating officer post was a particularly crucial (and difficult) position to fill. It took

Graham a long time to find the right person for the role. She was demanding and not shy about making personnel changes, and had fired four COOs during the 1970s before finding Simmons. Over the next ten years, he would proceed to dramatically tighten operations and improve margins at both the newspaper and the broadcasting divisions.

Simmons shared Graham's bias toward decentralization, and with her support, wasted little time in putting the right people in key seats at the operating divisions. He also gave his managers great autonomy and tied their compensation to performance relative to peers'.

The Post Company had a historical bias toward decentralization and lean corporate staffing that went back to Eugene Meyer and Phil Graham, both of whom were highly confident in their own judgment and did not feel the need to surround themselves with many advisers. This tendency would become more professionalized and pronounced under Katharine Graham and Simmons. Graham worked hard to identify the best people and then was very comfortable leaving them alone. Her son Donald, under the influence of Buffett and Dan Burke, would continue and extend his mother's historical emphasis on decentralization. He told me that today, he believes, "The Post Company is one of the most decentralized businesses in the country."

Having watched her father hand over day-to-day management of the paper to her thirty-one-year-old husband, Graham was also unafraid to give responsibility to promising managers at very young ages. Tom Might, who would later run the company's cable operations brilliantly, was given responsibility for the largest capital project in the company's history, a new printing plant in

Springfield, Virginia, at age thirty (he would bring it in 30 percent under budget). Alan Spoon was made COO of the company at thirty-nine, Jonathan Grayer was made CEO of the education division at twenty-nine, and Donald was made publisher of the *Post* at thirty-three.

. . .

Despite her success, Graham was plagued by occasional bouts of self-doubt well into her nearly thirty-year tenure as CEO. Fortunately, she was also strong willed, independent, and comfortable making controversial, unconventional decisions whether they involved refusing the demands of recalcitrant strikers, not buckling under to repeated threats from the Nixon administration, or ignoring other newspaper executives when they questioned her obsession with buying her own stock and her timidity in making acquisitions. In the end, this neophyte CEO left a journalistic and financial legacy that would be the envy of her peers, and she did it with great style and panache. As Ben Bradlee told me with a wistful grin, "She was just so much *fun*."[9]

## Postscript: A Tale of Two Companies

It would be hard to find a business that has had a more dramatic fall from grace over the last twenty years than the newspaper business. Once Warren Buffett's paragon of an impregnable, "wide-moat" business with unassailable competitive advantages in local advertising markets, the business has long been in secular decline, with the largest papers struggling to remain profitable in the face of new competition for advertising from online players like Google. Several sizable chains declared bankruptcy over the last several years, and the industry's stock prices have reflected this long and dramatic decline, falling over 60 percent in the last eight years.

The Post Company, under Donald Graham's leadership, has certainly not been immune to these secular headwinds. It has still, however, managed to outperform its peers, losing only 40 percent of its value over the same period, thanks to generally strong performances from its nonpublishing businesses.

Again, CEOs can only play the hands they are dealt, and Donald Graham, as the CEO of a large newspaper company, was dealt tough cards (although thanks to his mother's diversification efforts, significantly better ones than his peers'). He has, however, played them substantially better than his peers by adhering to the tenets of his mother's approach: making selected acquisitions, aggressively and opportunistically repurchasing stock (including *20 percent* of shares outstanding between 2009 and 2011), and keeping dividend levels relatively low.

In contrast, over the same period, the other well-known, publicly traded, family-owned Northeastern newspaper company—the Sulzbergers' New York Times Company—overpaid for an Internet portal (Ask.com), built an elaborate new corporate headquarters building in midtown Manhattan . . . and lost almost 90 percent of its value.

## CHAPTER 6

# A Public LBO

## *Bill Stiritz and Ralston Purina*

Should you find yourself in a chronically leaking boat, energy devoted to changing vessels is likely to be more productive than energy devoted to patching leaks.

—*Warren Buffett*

For most of the last fifty years, the large packaged goods companies, including household names such as Campbell Soup, Heinz, and Kellogg, were considered the bluest of blue-chip stocks for their attractive combination of predictable growth, recession resistance, and reliable dividends. These companies had long been paragons of financial conservatism, using little leverage, reliably paying dividends, and rarely repurchasing shares. Most of them had followed fashion and actively diversified during the 1960s and 1970s in the quixotic pursuit of synergy, and many had ended up in restaurant and agricultural businesses in search of the elusive benefits of "vertical integration."

Ralston Purina was fairly typical of this group. In the early 1980s, Ralston was a *Fortune* 100 company with a long history in agricultural feed products. During the 1970s under CEO Hal Dean, the company had followed the same path as its peers, taking the enormous cash flow provided by its traditional feed businesses and engaging in a diversification program that left it with a melange of operating divisions, ranging from mushroom and soybean farms to the Jack in the Box chain of fast-food restaurants, the St. Louis Blues hockey team, and the Keystone ski resort in Colorado. When Dean announced his retirement in 1980, the company's stock price had not moved in a decade.

After Dean's announcement, Ralston's board conducted a thorough search for his replacement, involving a wide slate of internal and external candidates. As the search unfolded, a number of top national candidates emerged (including Tom Wyman, later CEO of CBS). Late in the process, a lesser-known candidate—a longtime company man who was not even the lead internal candidate—improved his chances dramatically when he submitted an unsolicited memo to the board outlining in detail his strategy for the company. After reading it, influential director Mary Wells Lawrence (founder of the Wells, Rich, Greene advertising agency) telegrammed back, "*bullseye.*" Within days, that candidate, Bill Stiritz, had the job.

. . .

Bill Stiritz's career trajectory differs from that of the other CEOs in this book. He was an insider, having spent seventeen years at

Ralston before becoming CEO at the age of forty-seven. This seemingly conventional background, however, masked a fiercely independent cast of mind that made him a highly effective, if unlikely, change agent. When Stiritz assumed the CEO role, it would have been impossible to predict the radical transformation he would effect at Ralston and the broader influence it would have on his peers in the food and packaged goods industries.

Stiritz had an unusual educational background for a CEO. He had an interrupted undergraduate experience, attending the University of Arkansas for only a year before leaving for a four-year stint in the navy when his funds ran out. During his years in the navy, he honed the poker skills that would eventually pay for his college tuition. After the navy, he returned to college, completing his degree at Northwestern, where he majored in business studies. He never earned an MBA. Repeatedly labeled "cerebral" by his colleagues and Wall Street analysts, he did, however, receive a master's degree in European history from Saint Louis University in his mid-thirties.

After Northwestern, he had worked at the Pillsbury Company, starting as a field rep placing cereal on store shelves in northern Michigan (one of his largest accounts was an Indian reservation). Stiritz believes this grassroots experience was essential in helping him understand the nuts and bolts of distribution channels. He was subsequently promoted to product manager, a position that gave him broader exposure to consumer packaged goods (CPG) marketing. Wanting to understand media and advertising better, he left after two years for the Gardner Advertising agency in St. Louis. At Gardner, he showed an early interest in quantitative approaches to marketing and was a pioneering user of the nascent Nielsen ratings service, which helped give him a detailed understanding of the relationship between market share and promotional spending.

Stiritz joined Ralston Purina in 1964 at age thirty and was assigned to the grocery products division (pet food and cereals), long considered the "redheaded stepchild" within Ralston's large portfolio of businesses. He worked there for several years in positions of increasing responsibility, becoming general manager of the division in 1971. During his tenure, the business grew dramatically, with operating profits increasing *fiftyfold* through a relentless program of new product introductions and line extensions.

Stiritz personally oversaw the introduction of Purina Puppy and Cat Chow, two of the most successful launches in the history of the pet food industry. For a marketer, Stiritz was highly analytical, with a natural facility for numbers and a skeptical, almost prickly temperament. These traits had helped him at the poker table and would serve him well as CEO.

. . .

On assuming the CEO role in 1981, Stiritz wasted little time in aggressively restructuring the company. He fully appreciated the exceptionally attractive economics of the company's portfolio of consumer brands and promptly reorganized the company around these businesses, which he believed offered an attractive combination of high margins and low capital requirements. He immediately began to remove the underpinnings of his predecessor's strategy, and his first moves involved actively divesting businesses that did not meet his criteria for profitability and returns.

In his early years at the helm, Stiritz sold the Jack in the Box chain of fast-food restaurants, the mushroom farms, and the St. Louis Blues hockey franchise. The sale of the Blues in particular put Wall Street and the local business community on alert that the new CEO would be taking a radically different approach to managing Ralston.

Stiritz proceeded to sell other noncore businesses, including the company's soybean operations and miscellaneous restaurant and food service operations, leaving Ralston as a pure branded products company. In this regard, he was not unlike Warren Buffett in the early days at Berkshire Hathaway, extracting capital from the low-return textile business to deploy in much higher-return insurance and media businesses.

Starting in the early 1980s, Stiritz overcame initial board resistance and initiated an aggressive stock repurchase program. He was alone among the major branded products companies in pursuing buybacks, which he believed could generate compelling returns, and they would remain a central tenet of his capital allocation plan for the remainder of his tenure.

Starting in the mid-1980s, after the initial round of divestitures, Stiritz made two large acquisitions totaling a combined 30 percent of Ralston's enterprise value, both of them largely financed with debt. The first added Continental Baking, the maker of Twinkies and Wonder Bread, to Ralston's stable of brands. Stiritz bought Continental from the diversified conglomerate ITT, where it had languished as the company's lone packaged goods business. Under Ralston's management, distribution was expanded, redundant costs were eliminated, new products were introduced, and cash flow grew significantly, creating significant value for shareholders.

Next, in 1986, Stiritz made his largest purchase ever, acquiring the Energizer Battery division from Union Carbide for $1.5 billion, equal to 20 percent of Ralston's enterprise value. Union Carbide was struggling in the wake of the Bhopal disaster, and its battery business, despite a strong brand name, had long been a neglected, noncore operation. Like ITT, Union Carbide was a motivated seller lacking in consumer products marketing expertise. Stiritz prevailed in an auction, paying an admittedly full price for an asset he felt had a uniquely attractive combination of a growing duopoly market and undermanaged operations.

As he had at Continental, Stiritz moved immediately to improve Energizer's products and marketing (including the creation of the famous ad campaign featuring the eponymous bunny), enhance distribution, and eliminate excess costs. With this series of actions, the first step in Stiritz's transformation of Ralston was complete. By the late 1980s, the percentage of Ralston's revenues coming from consumer packaged goods had risen to almost 90 percent.

This transformation had a remarkable effect on the company's key operating metrics. As the business mix at Ralston shifted toward branded products, pretax profit margins grew from 9 percent to 15 percent, and return on equity more than doubled, from 15 percent to 37 percent. When combined with a shrinking share base, this produced exceptional growth in earnings per share and returns to shareholders.

Throughout the balance of the 1980s, Stiritz continued to optimize his portfolio of brands, making selected divestitures and add-on acquisitions. Businesses that could not generate acceptable returns were sold (or closed). These divestitures included underperforming food brands (including the Van de Kamp's frozen seafood division, a rare acquisition mistake) and the company's legacy agricultural feed business, Purina Mills, which had become a commodity business with chronic low returns and limited growth prospects. His add-on acquisitions focused on the core battery and pet food brands, particularly in underpenetrated international markets. All these decisions were guided by a careful analysis of potential returns for shareholders.

Throughout the 1990s, Stiritz focused on continued opportunistic stock buybacks, occasional acquisitions, and, significantly, the use of a relatively new structuring device, the spin-off, to rationalize Ralston's brand portfolio. Stiritz came to believe that even with a relatively decentralized corporate structure, some of the company's businesses were not receiving the attention they deserved either internally or from Wall Street. To rectify this and to minimize taxes, Stiritz became an early user of spin-offs.

In a spin-off, a business unit is transferred from the parent company into a new corporate entity. Shareholders in the parent company are given equivalent pro rata ownership in the new company and can make their own decisions about whether to hold or sell these shares. Importantly, spin-offs highlight the value of smaller business units, allow for better alignment of management incentives, and, critically, defer capital gains taxes.

Stiritz began this program with the 1994 spin-off of a collection of smaller brands, including Chex cereals and the ski resorts, into a new entity, Ralcorp. He remained the chairman of the new entity, which had a separate board and two co-CEOs. Stiritz would continue to rationalize and optimize Ralston's portfolio with the 1998 sale of the company's remaining agricultural businesses (including the fast-growing protein technology business) for a record price to DuPont in a stock deal (again avoiding capital gains taxes).

His last move (and the largest by far) was the spin-off of Energizer Holdings in 2000, which at the time had an enterprise value equal to 15 percent of the company's total value. These spin-offs have all performed exceptionally well as independent publicly traded companies (Ralcorp, originally a collection of neglected assets, today has an enterprise value of $5 billion).

This series of moves left Ralston at the dawn of the new millennium as a pure play pet food company, the dominant player by far in the US market. It did not escape Stiritz's attention that pruning unrelated businesses might make the company's core pet food brands more attractive to a strategic acquirer, and in 2001 the company was approached by Nestlé. After extensive negotiations (which Stiritz characteristically handled himself), the Swiss giant agreed to pay a record price for Ralston: $10.4 billion, equal to an extraordinary multiple of fourteen times cash flow. This transaction was the capstone of Stiritz's tenure at Ralston.

During a period when all of his peers had excellent returns, Stiritz's numbers were exceptional. Over his nineteen years at the helm, Stiritz's transformation of Ralston into a streamlined packaged goods company had a propulsive effect on the company's stock price. As figure 6-1 shows, a dollar invested with Stiritz when he became CEO was worth $57 nineteen years later, a compound return of *20.0 percent,* comfortably surpassing both his peers (*17.7 percent*) and the S&P (*14.7 percent*).

**FIGURE 6-1**

## Ralston Purina value of $1

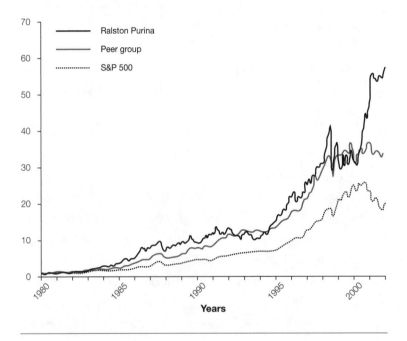

### The Nuts and Bolts

Michael Mauboussin, now a well-respected investor at Legg Mason, covered Stiritz and Ralston Purina as his first research assignment at Drexel Burnham in the mid-1980s. He became fascinated by Ralston's maverick CEO and did an early comprehensive research report on the company, building on the work of his mentor, Alan Greditor, a rare Wall Street analyst whom Stiritz respected. With Greditor's coaching, Mauboussin came to appreciate Stiritz's unique approach to capital allocation.

When asked to summarize what made Stiritz different, Mauboussin told me, "Effective capital allocation . . . requires a certain temperament. To be successful you have to think like an investor, dispassionately and probabilistically, with a certain coolness. Stiritz had that mindset."[1]

Stiritz himself likened capital allocation to poker, in which the key skills were an ability to calculate odds, read personalities, and make large bets when the odds were overwhelmingly in your favor. He was an active acquirer who was also comfortable selling or spinning off businesses that he felt were mature or underappreciated by Wall Street.

As longtime Goldman Sachs analyst Nomi Ghez emphasized to me, the food business had traditionally been a very profitable, predictable business generally characterized by low growth. Alone among public company CEOs, Stiritz saw this combination of characteristics and arrived at a new approach for optimizing shareholder value. In fact, he fundamentally changed the paradigm by actively deploying leverage to achieve substantially higher returns on equity, pruning less profitable businesses, acquiring related businesses, and actively repurchasing shares. In doing this, he was echoing the techniques of the pioneering private equity firms, including Kohlberg Kravis Roberts (KKR), which had successfully targeted underperforming packaged goods companies (Beatrice Foods and later RJR Nabisco) for some of the largest early leveraged buyouts (LBOs). (In fact, Stiritz was an underbidder on both Beatrice and RJR. He also made unsuccessful bids for Gillette and Gatorade.)

. . .

The primary sources of funds at Ralston during Stiritz's tenure were internal cash flow, debt, and, particularly in the early years, proceeds from asset sales.

Operating cash flow was a significant and growing source of funds throughout Stiritz's time at the helm. Margins steadily improved under his management, reflecting both a shifting mix toward branded products and a leaner, more decentralized operating philosophy. By the time of the Nestlé sale, Ralston's margins were the highest in the packaged goods industry.

Stiritz was the pioneer among consumer packaged goods CEOs in the use of debt. This was heresy in an industry that had long been characterized by exceptionally conservative financial management. Stiritz, however, saw that the prudent use of leverage could enhance shareholders' returns significantly. He believed that businesses with predictable cash flows should employ debt to enhance shareholder returns, and he made active use of leverage to finance stock repurchases and acquisitions, including his two largest, Energizer and Continental. Ralston consistently maintained an industry-high average debt–to–cash flow ratio during his tenure, as figure 6-2 shows.

Stiritz's approach to sales and divestitures evolved over time. He started by selling noncore businesses, like the mushroom farms and the hockey team, that did not meet his criteria for profitability and returns, and these asset sales were an important early source of cash for the company. In this regard, there were no sacred cows (including the ancestral feed business). "Stiritz knew what things were worth and would sell any asset for the right price," Mauboussin told me approvingly.[2] During this period, he

**FIGURE 6-2**

## Ralston's debt levels were consistently above competitors'

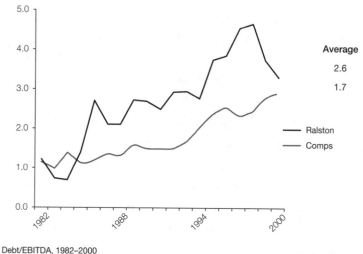

Debt/EBITDA, 1982–2000

*Source:* Center for Research in Security Prices (CRSP) and company filings.

*Note:* Debt-to-EBITDA calculated as EBITDA / (notes payable + current portion of long-term debt + long-term debt).

was focused on divesting noncore assets at the best possible prices and redeploying the capital into higher-return packaged goods businesses like Energizer and the Continental Baking brands.

However, Stiritz eventually developed an appreciation for the tax inefficiency of asset sales and, as we've seen, began to use spin-offs, which he believed released entrepreneurial energy and creativity while deferring capital gains taxes. From the outset, Stiritz had been a believer in decentralization, working to reduce layers of corporate bureaucracy and giving responsibility and autonomy for the company's key businesses to a close-knit group of managers. He viewed spin-offs as a further move in this direction, "the ultimate decentralization," providing managers and shareholders with an attractive combination of transparency and autonomy and allowing managers to be compensated more directly on their operating results than was possible in the larger conglomerated structure of the mother company.

Stiritz also proved to be a very astute seller. After his initial flurry of divestitures in the early 1980s, he made only two asset sales, both of them large. The first was the sale to DuPont of Ralston's protein business. DuPont paid a very high price for this business, and Stiritz opted to take stock, thus deferring capital gains taxes. The other divestiture was the Nestlé sale, which, as we've seen, resulted in a record price of over $10 billion. While Stiritz acknowledges today that the price was very attractive, he regrets not taking stock, given the strength of Nestlé's business and the capital gains tax incurred by his shareholders.

.  .  .

Outside of the steady, year-in, year-out pattern of debt service, internal capital expenditures, and (minimal) dividends, Stiritz's two primary uses of cash were share repurchases and acquisitions. His approach to both was opportunistic in the extreme.

Stiritz was *the* pioneer in the consumer packaged goods business when it came to stock buybacks. In the early 1980s, when he started to repurchase stock, buybacks were still unusual and controversial; as one of Ralston's directors said at the time, "Why would you want to shrink the company. Aren't there any worthwhile growth initiatives?" Stiritz, in contrast, believed that repurchases were the highest-probability investments he could make, and after convincing his board to support him, he became an active repurchaser. He would eventually repurchase a phenomenal 60 percent of Ralston's shares, second only to Henry Singleton among the CEOs in this book, and he would earn very attractive returns on these buybacks, averaging a long-term internal rate of return of 13 percent.

He was, however, a very frugal buyer, preferring opportunistic open-market purchases to larger tenders that might raise the stock price prematurely. These purchases were consistently made when P/E multiples were at cyclical low points. (Stiritz even personally negotiated discounted brokerage rates for these buybacks.)

Stiritz believed buyback returns represented a handy benchmark for other internal capital investment decisions, particularly acquisitions. As his longtime lieutenant, Pat Mulcahy, said, "The hurdle we always used for investment decisions was the share repurchase return. If an acquisition, with some certainty, could beat that return, it was worth doing."[3] Conversely, if a potential acquisition's returns didn't meaningfully exceed the buyback return, Stiritz passed.

In his approach to acquisitions, Stiritz always sought an edge and focused on buying businesses that he believed could be improved by Ralston's marketing expertise and distribution clout. He preferred companies that had been undermanaged by prior owners; and, not coincidentally, his two largest acquisitions, Continental Baking and Energizer, were both small, neglected divisions within giant conglomerates. The long-term returns from these two purchases were excellent, with Energizer generating a *21 percent* compound return over fourteen years and Continental generating a *13 percent* return over an eleven-year holding period.

Stiritz focused on sourcing acquisitions through direct contact with sellers, avoiding competitive auctions whenever possible. The Continental Baking acquisition was sourced from a letter he sent directly to ITT chairman Rand Araskog, thus circumventing an auction.

Stiritz believed that Ralston should only pursue opportunities that presented compelling returns under conservative assumptions, and he disdained the false precision of detailed financial models, focusing instead on a handful of key variables: market growth, competition, potential operating improvements, and, always, cash generation. As he told me, "I really only cared about the key assumptions going into the model. First, I wanted to know about the underlying trends in the market: its growth and competitive dynamics."[4]

His protégé, Pat Mulcahy, who would later run the business, described Stiritz's approach to the seminal Energizer acquisition: "When the opportunity to buy Energizer came up, a small group of us met at 1:00 PM and got the seller's books. We performed a back of the envelope LBO model, met again at 4:00 PM and decided to bid $1.4 billion. Simple as that. We knew what we needed to focus on. No massive studies and no bankers."[5] Again, Stiritz's approach (similar to those of Tom Murphy, John Malone, Katharine Graham, and others) featured a single sheet of paper and an intense focus on key assumptions, *not* a forty-page set of projections.

. . .

Stiritz, aware of the early LBOs in the packaged goods industry, consciously adopted a private equity–like mind-set. His managerial worldview was neatly summarized by Mulcahy: "Stiritz ran Ralston somewhat akin to an LBO. He was one of the first to see the benefit to shareholders of higher leverage as long as cash flows were strong and predictable . . . He simply got rid of businesses that were cash drains (no matter their provenance) . . . and invested more deeply in existing strong businesses through massive share purchases interspersed with the occasional acquisition that met our return targets."[6]

Stiritz married nuts-and-bolts packaged goods marketing expertise with financial acumen, an unusual combination. He focused on newfangled metrics, like EBITDA and internal rate of return (IRR), that were becoming the lingua franca of the nascent private equity industry, and he eschewed more traditional accounting measures, such as reported earnings and book value, that were Wall Street's preferred financial metrics at the time. He had particular disdain for book value, once declaring during a rare appearance at an industry conference that "book equity has no meaning in our business," a statement that was greeted with stunned silence by the audience, according to longtime analyst John Bierbusse. Mauboussin added, "You have to have fortitude to look past book value, EPS, and other standard accounting metrics which don't always correlate with economic reality."[7]

. . .

Stiritz was fiercely independent, and actively disdained the advice of outside advisers. He believed that charisma was overrated as a managerial attribute and that analytical skill was a critical prerequisite for a CEO and the key to independent thinking: "Without it, chief executives are at the mercy of their bankers and CFOs." Stiritz observed that many CEOs came from functional areas (legal, marketing, manufacturing, sales) where this sort of analytical ability was not required. Without it, he believed they were severely handicapped. His counsel was simple: "Leadership is analysis."

This independent mind-set translated into an innate suspicion bordering on distrust of outside advisers, particularly investment bankers, whom Stiritz once described as "parasitic." He was surgical in his use of advisers—using as few as possible, always in a carefully targeted manner—and he was aggressive in negotiating their fees, holding up the multibillion-dollar Nestlé deal when he felt the bankers were overcharging him. He made a point of using different bankers for various transactions so that none felt overly secure about his business.

He was well known for showing up alone to important due diligence meetings or negotiations where the other side of the table was crowded with bankers and lawyers. Stiritz relished this unorthodox approach. A then junior banker at Goldman Sachs told me of a late-night due diligence session during the RJR Nabisco sale process when Stiritz came to a conference room at the Goldman offices alone, armed only with a yellow legal pad, and proceeded to walk through the key operating assumptions one by one before making a final bid and going to bed. He actively enjoyed the investment process and, after selling Ralston, vigorously managed an investment partnership consisting primarily of his own capital.

. . .

Stiritz jealously guarded his time, eschewing high-visibility, time-consuming philanthropic boards, and avoiding casual lunches as "mostly a waste of time." As he explained, "It got to the point where they were taking up too much time, so I stopped them completely." He did, however, make time to sit on other corporate boards, viewing this as a unique opportunity to expose himself to new situations and ideas.

He was always a fox-like sponge for new thinking regardless of its origin. John McMillin, a longtime industry analyst, once wrote, "Some people are innovators and some people borrow ideas from others. Stiritz is both (and that's meant as a compliment)."[8] He consciously carved out blocks of time in his schedule to wrestle with the key issues in the business alone, without distraction, whether on a Florida beach or in his home office in St. Louis.

He avoided time-consuming interactions with Wall Street and retained, in the words of analyst John Bierbusse, "a certain Garbo-like quality," rarely speaking to analysts, virtually never attending conferences, and never issuing quarterly guidance.[9]

. . .

By the mid- to late 1990s, Stiritz's heresy had become orthodoxy, and virtually all his peers had implemented different versions of his strategy: divesting noncore assets, repurchasing shares, and acquiring businesses complementary to their core product lines. Not surprisingly, in 2001, just as his strategy had gained wide industry acceptance and with packaged goods multiples at an all-time high, Stiritz abruptly changed course and sold Ralston to Nestlé for a record price, once again leaving his bewildered competitors scratching their heads.

## A Recent Example: Sara Lee

The flattery of imitation by industry peers continues to this day, over thirty years after Stiritz took the helm at Ralston. The latest, and maybe last, of the consumer products companies to follow in Stiritz's footsteps is Sara Lee, which over the last five years, under the leadership of CEOs Brenda Barnes and Marcel Smits, has sold off noncore operations, bought back 13 percent of its shares, maintained a relatively high level of leverage, and generated returns for shareholders that have dwarfed its peer group. As of this writing, Sara Lee had recently declined a purchase offer for the entire company from a consortium of private equity firms at a meaningful premium to the company's prior stock price. Instead, the company announced it would spin off its highly profitably coffee and tea operations and pay a sizable onetime dividend. Sound familiar?

## CHAPTER 7

# Optimizing the Family Firm

## *Dick Smith and General Cinema*

It's remarkable how much value can be created by a small group of really talented people.

—*David Wargo, Putnam Investments*

In 1962, Phillip Smith died suddenly of a heart attack. Smith had come to Boston from Russia in 1908 and, after working a variety of odd jobs, had found his way into the nascent nickelodeon business. He worked first as an usher, advanced to ticket taker, and was eventually promoted to general manager of a movie theater in downtown Boston. In 1922, five years before Al Jolson broke the cinematic sound barrier, he borrowed money from friends and family and opened a theater in Boston's North End.

Over the following forty years, Smith built a successful chain of theaters, starting in New England and then expanding into the

Midwest. He was a pioneer of the drive-in movie theater, and he developed a reputation as a savvy operator. A year earlier, in 1961, he had taken the company public to raise capital to build additional drive-ins. After Smith's untimely death at the age of sixty-two, his son Dick immediately took over as CEO of General Drive-In, as the company was then known. He was thirty-seven years old.

Over the ensuing forty-three years, starting with this unexceptional chain of movie theaters, this neophyte CEO simply thrashed the broader market and Jack Welch with a remarkable cumulative outperformance versus the S&P of over *eleven times*. Dick Smith achieved these results in the context of a publicly traded firm that was controlled by its founding family. He ran the company as though it were privately held and demonstrated unique patience in deploying the company's cash flow to diversify away from the maturing drive-in business, first into shopping mall theaters and then into entirely different business lines.

Smith would alternate long periods of inactivity with the occasional very large transaction. During his tenure, he would make three significant acquisitions (one in the late 1960s, one in the mid-1980s, and one in the early 1990s) in unrelated businesses: soft drink bottling (American Beverage Company), retailing (Carter Hawley Hale), and publishing (Harcourt Brace Jovanovich). This series of transactions transformed the regional drive-in company into an enormously successful consumer conglomerate.

The business world is strewn with the wreckage of companies that tried unsuccessfully to purchase businesses outside of their industry. Such diversifying acquisitions are notoriously difficult to execute (think Time Warner and AOL), and yet Smith, a relatively inexperienced nepotism beneficiary, became a master of them. In fact, his tenure at General Cinema can be seen as an extended process of serial reinvention. It is also the story of a series of extraordinarily well-timed exits, one in the late 1980s and one each in 2003 and 2006. This accordion-like pattern of expansion and contraction, of diversification and divestiture, was highly unusual (although similar in some ways to Henry Singleton's at Teledyne) and paid enormous benefits for General Cinema's shareholders.

. . .

Dick Smith was born in Newton, Massachusetts, in 1924. He was the eldest son in a close-knit family of four and from a very early age, worked weekends and vacations in the family business. He went to prep school in Cambridge and graduated from Harvard College with an engineering degree in 1946. He worked as a naval engineer during World War II and after the war, eschewed an MBA to go back to work in the family business. In 1956, when Smith was thirty-two, his father made him a full partner.

After his father's death, Smith worked to aggressively expand the company's theater circuit into suburban shopping malls, where it was the unquestioned pioneer. Smith was the first in the industry to recognize that suburban theaters were the beneficiaries of strong, underlying demographic trends, and in moving to capture this opportunity, he developed two revolutionary new practices.

The first was in the area of new theater financing. The traditional approach to theater development had emphasized ownership of the underlying land, allowing for long-term control of assets and access to mortgage financing. Smith, however, realized that a well-located theater could quickly generate predictable cash flow, and he pioneered the use of lease financing to build new theaters, dramatically reducing up-front investment. This innovation allowed Smith to grow General Cinema's theater circuit rapidly with minimal capital investment.

His second innovation was to add more screens per theater to attract larger audiences and to optimize high-margin concession sales. As a result of these dual innovations, General Cinema enjoyed exceptional returns on its investments in new theaters throughout the 1960s and into the early 1970s. By the late 1960s, however, Smith, realizing that theater growth was unlikely to continue indefinitely, began to explore diversification into new businesses that offered better long-term prospects.

The transformational acquisition for Smith was the 1968 purchase of the Ohio-based American Beverage Company (ABC), the largest, independent Pepsi bottler in the country. Smith was familiar with the beverage business through his involvement with theater concessions, and when he learned that ABC might be for sale, he moved quickly. The deal as negotiated by Smith was both compelling (an attractive price of five times cash flow) and very large, equaling over 20 percent of the company's enterprise value (EV) at the time. Smith leveraged his real estate expertise to creatively finance the purchase via a sale/leaseback of ABC's manufacturing facilities (he is still justifiably proud of this coup).

Smith had grown up in the bricks-and-mortar world of movie theaters, and ABC was his first exposure to the value of businesses with intangible assets, like beverage brands. Smith grew to love the beverage business, which was an oligopoly with very high returns on capital and attractive long-term growth trends. He particularly liked the dynamics within the Pepsi bottler universe, which was fragmented and had many second- and third-generation owners who were potential sellers (unlike the Coke system, which was dominated by a smaller number of large independents). Because Pepsi was the number two brand, its franchises often traded at lower valuations than Coke's.

In buying ABC, Smith acquired a legitimate *platform company*—one that other companies could be added to easily and efficiently. As ABC developed scale advantages, Smith realized he could purchase new franchises at seemingly high multiples of the seller's cash flow and immediately reduce the effective price through expense reduction, tax savvy, and marketing expertise. Acting on this insight, Smith aggressively acquired other franchises, including American Pepsi in 1973, Pepsi Cola Bottling Company in 1977, and the Washington, DC, franchise in 1977.

As in the theater business, Smith and his team were innovative marketers and efficient operators. The company constantly sought to reduce costs, using its scale to reduce can pricing and purchasing sugar directly in international markets to avoid the parent company's markup. As a result, ABC had industry-leading margins. In addition to Pepsi franchises, Smith occasionally bought other beverage (7 Up and Dr Pepper) franchises, and in 1976, the company partnered with the largest orange grower's co-op to create Sunkist orange soda, which they rolled out through their distribution network. ABC eventually invested $20 million to launch Sunkist, and in 1984 sold it to Canada Dry for $87 million, generating an exceptional return on investment.

After the beverage business was established, Smith began to look for another business that could add a "third leg" to the General Cinema stool. Along these lines, in the late 1970s and early 1980s, the company made a number of smaller acquisitions in the broadcast media business, buying several TV and radio stations. Smith's price discipline, however, prevented General Cinema from paying the double-digit multiples then prevalent in the broadcast industry. Although it earned very good returns on its small portfolio of media investments, the company never became a major player—"a missed opportunity," according to longtime investor Bob Beck of Putnam Investments.[1]

As time went on, Smith's approach to acquisitions evolved. From the early 1980s on, Smith and his team focused on the occasional, large opportunistic acquisition and on a series of minority investments in public companies that he believed to be undervalued. These investments were attempts at diversification through a strategy of what Smith termed *investment with involvement,* the idea being to make a sizable minority investment, take a seat on the board, and work with management to improve operations and increase value.

In the first half of the 1980s, Smith was involved with three of these investment-with-involvement attempts: Columbia Pictures, Heublein, and Cadbury Schweppes. In the case of the latter two, the incumbent management team viewed the General Cinema investment with suspicion or outright hostility. As a result, no board seats were offered, and Smith sold each of the positions within one to two years of the initial purchase. The returns from these investments were attractive, but the broader objective of diversification was not achieved. That changed suddenly in April 1985, when Woody Ives, the company's CFO, picked up his phone to find Morgan Stanley investment banker Eric Gleacher on the line with a potential "third leg."

. . .

Gleacher was calling about Carter Hawley Hale (CHH), a publicly traded retail conglomerate that owned several department store and specialty retail chains. Leslie Wexner, the CEO of The Limited, had recently made a hostile takeover bid for CHH, and Gleacher had been hired to find a "white knight," a friendly investor who could buy a significant percentage of the stock and thwart a takeover.

Ives had an initially cool reaction to Gleacher's description, but as he listened, he sensed a potentially significant opportunity. The timing was almost impossibly tight (they would need to respond by the following Tuesday), and Ives realized that any buyer who could perform to this unforgiving timetable would have enormous leverage in negotiating a transaction. Ives got off the phone and spoke to Dick Smith and the other top members of the management team. By 5 p.m. they were on a plane to CHH's corporate headquarters in Los Angeles.

They spent the weekend in intensive due diligence and negotiations and emerged Sunday evening with an agreement. On Monday (Patriots' Day, a bank holiday in Boston) they hastily assembled a syndicate of three banks to finance the transaction, and by Thursday, a week and a day after Gleacher's initial call, the deal had closed. Smith and his management team had so refined their acquisition criteria and process that they were able to perform to this extraordinary timetable. Very few publicly traded firms could have moved so quickly on such a large transaction.

The CHH investment is an excellent example of Smith's opportunism and his willingness to make sizable bets when circumstances warranted. The transaction was both very large (equal to over *40 percent* of GC's enterprise value) and very complex. It was also very attractive. Ives negotiated a preferred security that guaranteed General Cinema a 10 percent return, allowed it to convert its interest into 40 percent of the common stock if the business performed well, and included a fixed-price option to buy Waldenbooks, a wholly owned subsidiary of CHH. As Ives summarized to me, "At the end of the day, we borrowed money at 6–7 percent fully tax-deductible while earning 10 percent on tax advantaged debt, plus we got a conversion option (which eventually allowed us to peel off the Neiman Marcus Group) and the option to buy Waldenbooks."[2] Not a bad weekend's work.

Eventually General Cinema would exchange its 40 percent ownership in CHH shares for a controlling 60 percent stake in the company's specialty retail division, whose primary asset was the Neiman Marcus chain. The long-term returns on the company's CHH investment were an extraordinary 51.2 percent. The CHH transaction moved General Cinema decisively into retailing, a new business whose attractive growth prospects were not correlated with either the beverage or the theater businesses.

. . .

Smith saw two troubling trends emerging in the late 1980s: a newly rejuvenated Coke attacking Pepsi in local markets and a dramatic increase in the prices for beverage franchises as the industry's favorable economics became more widely appreciated. With reluctance, he responded by deciding to explore the sale of the business, eventually selling it in 1989 to the Pepsi parent company for a record price. Following this sale, General Cinema was left with over $1 billion in cash on its balance sheet, and Smith began to look again for a diversifying acquisition.

It didn't take him long to find one. In 1991, after a tortuous eighteen-month process, Smith made his largest and last acquisition, buying publisher Harcourt Brace Jovanovich (HBJ) in a complex auction process and assembling General Cinema's final third leg. HBJ was a leading educational and scientific publisher that also owned a testing business and an outplacement firm. Since the mid-1960s, the firm had been run as a personal fiefdom by CEO William Jovanovich. In 1986, the company received a hostile takeover bid from the renegade British publisher Robert Maxwell, and in response Jovanovich had taken on large amounts of debt, sold off HBJ's amusement park business, and made a large distribution to shareholders.

This series of moves kept Maxwell at bay but left the company with an unsustainable debt load. As the company tripped covenants and missed payments, its debt traded down to discounted levels, and several vulture investors (including Leon Black of Apollo Investments) began to accumulate positions in the company's complex layer cake of debt securities.

As operations stagnated, William Jovanovich retired and was replaced by his son, Peter, a longtime HBJ executive. In late 1990, the company hired Smith Barney to conduct a sale process. At General Cinema, the executive team dove in to analyze

HBJ's complex capital structure. Despite their aversion to auctions, the management team concluded that the business fit well with General Cinema's acquisition criteria, and they decided to aggressively pursue it.

They also believed that HBJ's byzantine balance sheet (characterized by investment banker Caesar Sweitzer as an "AP course in corporate finance") would likely deter other buyers, creating an opportunity for a nimble, well-capitalized independent buyer to negotiate an attractive valuation.[3] After extensive negotiations with the company's many debt holders, Smith agreed to purchase the company for $1.56 billion, which represented 62 percent of General Cinema's enterprise value at the time—an enormous bet. This price equaled a multiple of six times cash flow for HBJ's core publishing assets, an attractive price relative to comparable transactions (Smith would eventually sell those businesses for eleven times cash flow). Table 7-1 outlines the sources and uses for the transaction, giving a sense for its complexity and the number of parties involved.

Following the HBJ acquisition in 1991, General Cinema spun off its mature theater business into a separate publicly traded entity, GC Companies (GCC), allowing management to focus its attention on the larger retail and publishing businesses. Smith and his management team proceeded to operate both the retail and the publishing businesses over the next decade. In 2003, Smith sold the HBJ publishing assets to Reed Elsevier, and in 2006 he sold Neiman Marcus, the last vestige of the General Cinema portfolio, to a consortium of private equity buyers. Both transactions would set valuation records within their industries, capping an extraordinary run for Smith and General Cinema shareholders.

TABLE 7-1

**Financial data from General Cinema's acquisition of Harcourt Brace Jovanovich**

|  | Original offer | Final offer |
| --- | --- | --- |
|  | $1.46 billion | $1.56 billion |
| HBJ common stock | $1.30 in cash | $0.75 in GC stock |
| HBJ preferred stock | $1.30 in cash | $0.75 in GC stock |
| HBJ senior notes | 93% of principal | 100% of principal |
| HBJ senior sub debt | 77% | 91% |
| HBJ sub debt | 45% | 47.5% |
| HBJ zero coupons | 32.4% | 40.975% |
| HBJ PIKs | 40% | 47% |

*Source:* General Cinema/Harcourt Brace Jovanovich joint proxy statement, pp. 32, 40, 46–47.

Smith, thrust unexpectedly into the CEO spot by his father's death, posted extraordinary numbers over his forty-three years at the helm of General Cinema (see figure 7-1), generating a remarkable *16.1 percent* compound annual return for his shareholders, dwarfing the *9 percent* returns for the S&P and the *9.8 percent* returns for GE over the same period. A dollar invested with Dick Smith at the beginning of 1962 would have been worth *$684* at the end of the period. That same dollar invested in the S&P would have been worth $43, and $60 if invested with GE.

## The Nuts and Bolts

Smith evolved a distinctive approach to managing General Cinema's operations. He ran the company in close collaboration with

**FIGURE 7-1**

## Total shareholder return dramatically exceeded the S&P 500 and comparables' return

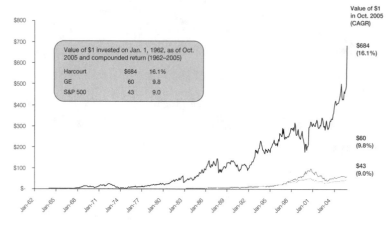

Total value of $1 invested in January 1962.[a]

*Source:* Center for Research in Security Prices (CRSP).

*Note:* NMG was spun off to GC shareholders in October 1989, and Harcourt General was sold to Reed Elsevier in July 2001. In order to capture the return generated from the sale of NMG to TPG and Warburg Pincus in October 2005, assume that proceeds from the sale to Reed Elsevier are reinvested in a security whose value grows each year at the average growth of Leucadia and the S&P 500 for that year (Leucadia and S&P CAGR of 17.7% and 0.7% over the period of July 2001–October 2005).

a. Assumes that dividends (taxed at 35%) are reinvested upon receipt into common shares of the stock of the company.

a coterie of three top executives: chief financial officer Woody Ives, chief operating officer Bob Tarr, and corporate counsel Sam Frankenheim. He officially designated this group the Office of the Chairman, or the OOC. The OOC met weekly, and Smith actively encouraged debate among his top executives. Longtime General Cinema investment banker Caesar Sweitzer characterized these sessions as "wrestling matches conducted in a constructive, collegial way."[4]

Smith was even willing to be outvoted by the other OOC members. Woody Ives, the company's talented CFO, remembers one of his proudest moments at General Cinema (Ives later left to lead a successful turnaround at Eastern Resources), when a joint venture to enter the cable business with Comcast and CBS was shot down by the board after Smith let Ives voice a dissenting opinion: "He gave me permission to publicly disagree with him in front of the Board. Very few CEOs would have done that."[5]

General Cinema operated with a very lean corporate staff. The company had its corporate headquarters next to one of its theaters in the rear of a nondescript shopping mall in Chestnut Hill, Massachusetts. Smith proudly notes that this suburban office space was effectively rent free because the theater covered the rent expense for the entire complex. Smith delegated management of day-to-day operations to the OOC and the division heads, and spent little time on investor communications, which were "only adequate," according to Putnam analyst Bob Beck.[6] Instead, he spent the majority of his time on strategic and capital allocation issues.

The company was run very tightly by this small group of managers. David Wargo, a longtime media investor, shared a report with me that he wrote following a meeting with management immediately after the HBJ acquisition. What's striking in the report is the crispness of the presentation: the clearly laid-out rationale for the deal and the accompanying list of specific benchmarks and return objectives, with no excess verbiage. What's also noteworthy in hindsight is that the company hit or exceeded every one of its targets. As Wargo says of the General Cinema team, "It's remarkable how much value can be created by a small group of really talented people."[7]

Smith, who had become CEO in his late thirties, was comfortable giving executives responsibility early in their careers. In 1974, Smith hired Ives, a thirty-seven-year-old investment banker with no operating experience, as the company's CFO. Similarly, in 1978, he named Tarr, a thirty-four-year-old former submarine commander and Harvard MBA, president of the beverage division. Smith would later hire Paul Del Rossi, aged thirty-five, to run the company's theater business.

Compensation for top executives was, in Smith's words, "competitive but not extraordinary."[8] However, the company did offer equity to key managers through options and a generous stock purchase program in which the company matched employee investments up to a stated maximum level. The net effect of these initiatives, according to Woody Ives, was that the executive team "felt like owners . . . we were all shareholders and behaved as such."[9]

. . .

Smith's capital allocation record was excellent. The three primary sources of cash during Smith's long tenure were operating cash flow, long-term debt, and proceeds from the occasional large asset sale.

The movie theater business is characterized by exceptional cash flow characteristics due to its negative working capital needs (customers pay in advance, while the movie studios are paid ninety days in arrears for their films) and low capital requirements (once a theater is built, very little investment is required to maintain it). These attractive economics had a powerful effect on Dick Smith's business worldview, and from a very early point in the company's history, he focused on maximizing cash flow, not traditional earnings per share (EPS).

When I met with Smith in his office, he showed me the 1962 annual report, his first as CEO, in which he refers repeatedly to *cash earnings* (defined as net earnings plus depreciation) as the key metric in evaluating company performance, *not* net income. This may well be the first use in American business parlance of that now standard term. As longtime General Cinema CFO Woody Ives said, "Our focus was always on cash," and across Smith's tenure, the company consistently generated high levels of operating cash flow.[10]

Smith disdained equity offerings. In fact, he almost entirely avoided issuing equity from the time of the company's IPO until issuing a microscopic number of shares in 1991 to facilitate favorable tax treatment for the HBJ transaction. As he said to me, "We never issued any stock. I was like a feudal lord, holding onto the ancestral land!"

The company did, however, make strategic use of debt to fund acquisitions. Its two largest purchases, Carter Hawley Hale and Harcourt Brace Jovanovich, were entirely debt financed. As a result, from the mid-1980s on, the company consistently maintained debt-to-cash flow ratios of at least three times, leveraging equity returns and helping minimize taxes.

Tax minimization was another important source of funds at General Cinema and another area where the company had a differentiated approach. Smith, in particular, was a pioneer in this area. As the company's longtime tax adviser, Dick Denning, told me, "They were extraordinarily sophisticated . . . and not bashful about exploring and utilizing new tax ideas." The effectiveness of this tax planning can be seen in the company's low effective average tax rate of 33 percent over Smith's tenure (during which corporate tax rates averaged close to 50 percent).

As we've seen, it is rare for a CEO to sell a large division or business without pressure from outside shareholders. Dick Smith, however (like several of the CEOs in this book, including Bill Anders and Bill Stiritz), was an exceptional seller of businesses, three separate times selling large divisions for record-setting prices: the beverage business in 1989, HBJ's publishing business in 2003, and the Neiman Marcus Group (NMG) in 2006. In each case, when he saw a combination of dimming growth prospects and high valuations, he moved aggressively to sell, even if it meant substantially shrinking his company.

In 2006, in the most recent example, Smith saw that further expansion of the Neiman Marcus chain would be both capital intensive (additional new stores required $50 million each in capital) and operationally challenging. He also saw that private equity firms, flush with low-cost debt, were paying record prices for premier retail properties. He hired Goldman Sachs, and after a full auction, a consortium led by Texas Pacific Group (TPG) paid a record multiple of cash flow for the Neiman Marcus Group.

The one maturing business that Smith didn't sell was the legacy General Cinema movie theater business, GC Companies. By the late 1990s, the movie exhibition business had become much more competitive. Rather than sell the theater division (Smith supposedly had an attractive offer for it in the late 1980s), the company attempted to rationalize its existing circuit to compete with the new megaplexes sprouting up around the country. It closed some theaters, expanded others, invested in new projection technology—all to no avail. By the late 1990s, GCC was no longer able to support its debt obligations and declared bankruptcy, a rare setback for Smith.

. . .

Smith deployed the cash provided by these various sources into three principal outlets: acquisitions, stock repurchases, and capital expenditures. The company paid minimal dividends and was notable for its willingness to hold large cash balances while waiting for attractive investment opportunities to emerge.

Smith's acquisitions shared several common characteristics. They were market leaders with solid growth prospects and respected brand names. They were also typically opportunistic transactions whose circumstances deterred other potential buyers—in the case of Carter Hawley Hale, no other buyer could have moved as quickly to counter The Limited's takeover bid; in the case of HBJ, no other purchaser was willing to spend the time to unravel the complex capital structure and negotiate with the manifold layers of debt holders. They were also very large bets relative to the company's size, ranging from 22 percent to a remarkable 62 percent of the company's enterprise value at the time they were made.

Smith was a steady repurchaser of General Cinema's stock over time, eventually buying back one-third of the company's shares. His long-term internal rate of return on these buybacks was a very attractive *16 percent*. When Heublein responded to the company's investment-with-involvement initiative in 1982 by buying a big block of GC's shares, Smith responded by buying back 10 percent of his own shares, his largest single repurchase.

General Cinema maintained a disciplined approach to capital expenditures, with all capital requests requiring attractive cash

returns on invested capital. The company's early suburban theaters generated exceptional returns, and the beverage division
also had attractive internal investment options. General Cinema's
other businesses were held to these high standards. The HBJ publishing business had very few physical assets and, as a result, low
capital requirements. The Neiman Marcus business, however,
had significant capital requirements.

Although the retail business was more capital intensive than
General Cinema's other businesses, Smith saw in Neiman Marcus
a unique brand that had been poorly run by its prior owners.
Smith was willing to make the occasional large investment to
open new Neiman stores because he believed that demonstrating
growth potential would allow the company to realize a premium
price on exit (in its twenty years of ownership, General Cinema
opened just twelve stores; the new buyer would plan to open
many times that number). This logic was amply justified by Neiman's stratospheric exit price.

. . .

As with Capital Cities, a sense of infectious enthusiasm perme-
ated my interviews with former top General Cinema executives,
a sense of camaraderie and adventure. Together, this group of
executives led the company into an eclectic succession of new
businesses. In each, they proved themselves to be exceptional operators with industry-leading margins and exceptional returns.
Smith succeeded in creating an environment where this talented
group of executives was given exceptional autonomy and felt like
owners. As Smith, with a gleam in his eye, summarized it to me,
"We all just had *so* much fun." As Woody Ives said of his personal
stock ownership, "I just wish I'd never sold a share."[11]

## CHAPTER 8

# The Investor as CEO

## *Warren Buffett and Berkshire Hathaway*

You shape your houses and then your houses shape you.

—*Winston Churchill*

The most powerful force in the universe is compound interest.

—*Albert Einstein*

Being a CEO has made me a better investor, and vice versa.

—*Warren Buffett*

Berkshire Hathaway, a one-hundred-year-old textile company located in New Bedford, Massachusetts, had been owned by the same two local families, the Chaces and the Stantons, for generations. The company, a vestige of the glory days of New England enterprise, was the unlikely target of an early hostile takeover in

1965—hostile, at least, to the company's stubborn septuagenarian CEO, Seabury Stanton. Stanton, by refusing to meet with a large, disgruntled investor, had created an unexpectedly formidable adversary.

The company was ultimately taken over, after an extended proxy fight, by this most unlikely raider—a little-known, jug-eared, thirty-five-year-old wunderkind from Nebraska named Warren Buffett. Buffett ran a small investment partnership out of a nondescript office building in Omaha and had no prior management experience.

He was very different from the notorious LBO barons of the 1980s, however. First of all, he was not very hostile, having established a close relationship with the Chace family before making his move. Second, he didn't use any debt—this was a long way from Gordon Gekko or Henry Kravis.

Buffett had been attracted to Berkshire by its cheap price relative to book value. At the time, the company had only a weak market position in a brutally competitive commodity business (suit linings) and a mere $18 million in market capitalization. From this undistinguished start, unprecedented results followed; and measured by long-term stock performance, the formerly crew-cut Nebraskan is simply on another planet from all other CEOs. These otherworldly returns had their origin in that aging New England textile company, which today has a market capitalization of $140 billion *and virtually the same number of shares.* Buffett bought his first share of Berkshire for $7; today it trades for over $120,000 a share.

How, from such an unlikely starting point, Buffett effected this remarkable transition and how his background as an investor shaped his unique approach to managing Berkshire is a compelling story.

. . .

Warren Buffett was born in 1930 in Omaha, Nebraska, where his family had deep roots. His grandfather ran a well-known local grocery store, and his father was a stockbroker in downtown Omaha and later a congressman. Buffett inherited their folksy personal style. He exhibited early entrepreneurial tendencies and pursued a variety of ventures, starting at the age of six and continuing through high school, including paper routes, vending machines, and soft drink reselling. After a brief stint at Wharton, he graduated from the University of Nebraska at age twenty and began to apply to business schools.

Buffett had always been interested in the stock market, and at age nineteen read a book called *The Intelligent Investor* by Benjamin Graham, which was a Paul-to-Damascus-type epiphany for him. Buffett was converted overnight into a value investor, following Graham's formula of buying companies that were statistically cheap, trading at significant discounts to net working capital ("net/nets," as they were known). He began to employ this strategy in investing the proceeds from his early business ventures (approximately $10,000 at the time), and after getting rejected by Harvard Business School, he went to Columbia to study with Graham. He became the star of Graham's class and received the first A+ the professor had awarded in his more than twenty years at Columbia.

After graduation in 1952, Buffett asked Graham for a job at his investment firm, but was turned down and returned to Omaha, where he took a job as a broker. The first company he recommended to clients was GEICO, a car insurance company that sold policies directly to government employees. The company had initially attracted Buffett's attention because Graham was its chairman, but the more he studied it, the more he realized GEICO had both important competitive advantages and a *margin of safety,* Graham's term for a price well below intrinsic value (the price a fully informed, sophisticated buyer would pay for the company). He invested the majority of his net worth in the company and attempted to interest his firm's clients in the stock. He found this a hard sell, however, and more generally found the brokerage business to be far removed from the investment research he had come to love.

He maintained contact with Graham during this period, constantly sending him stock ideas. Finally, in 1954, Graham relented and offered Buffett a job. Buffett moved back to New York and for the next two years worked for Graham researching net/nets (he later used the colorful analogy of "cigar butts" to describe these cheap, often low-quality, companies). In 1956, Graham dissolved his firm to focus on other interests (which included translating Aeschylus from ancient Greek), and Buffett returned to Omaha and raised a small ($105,000) investment partnership from friends and family. His own net worth had grown to $140,000 (over $1 million today).

Over the next thirteen years, Buffett achieved extraordinary results, materially beating the S&P every single year without employing leverage (see table 8-1). These results were generally achieved using Graham's deep value approach. Buffett, however, made two large investments in the mid-1960s, American Express

TABLE 8-1

## Buffett Partnership (percentage) results

|  | Buffett Partnership | Dow | Variance |
|---|---|---|---|
| 1957 | 10.4 | (8.4) | 18.8 |
| 1958 | 40.9 | 38.5 | 2.5 |
| 1959 | 25.9 | 20.6 | 5.3 |
| 1960 | 22.8 | (6.2) | 29.0 |
| 1961 | 45.9 | 22.4 | 23 |
| 1962 | 13.9 | (7.6) | 21 |
| 1963 | 38.7 | 20.6 | 18 |
| 1964 | 27.8 | 18.7 | 9 |
| 1965 | 47.2 | 14.2 | 33 |
| 1966 | 20.4 | (15.6) | 35 |
| 1967 | 35.9 | 19 | 14 |
| 1968 | 58.8 | 7.7 | 51 |
| 1969 | 6.8 | (11.6) | 18 |
| Average | 30.4 | 8.6 | 21.8 |

and Disney, that did not follow Graham's dictates and that presaged a larger shift in his investment philosophy toward higher-quality companies with strong competitive barriers.

In 1965, Buffett bought control of Berkshire Hathaway through the Buffett Partnership. He ran the partnership for four more years with continuing excellent results, and then in 1969 (not coincidentally, the same year Henry Singleton stopped making acquisitions at Teledyne), abruptly dissolved it in the face of the high prices of the late 1960s' bull market. He did, however, retain his ownership interest in Berkshire, seeing in it a potential future vehicle for his investment activity.

Immediately after buying control of Berkshire, Buffett installed a new CEO, Ken Chace. In the first three years under Chace's leadership, the company generated $14 million of cash as Chace reduced inventories and sold off excess plants and equipment, and the business experienced a (rare) cyclical burst of profitability. The lion's share of this capital was used to acquire National Indemnity, a niche insurance company that generated prodigious amounts of cash in the form of *float,* premium income generated in advance of losses and expenses. Buffett invested this float very effectively, buying both publicly traded securities and wholly owned businesses, including the *Omaha Sun,* a weekly newspaper in Omaha, and a bank in Rockford, Illinois.

Outside Berkshire Hathaway at the same time, Buffett began to work more closely with Charlie Munger, another Omaha native and a brilliant lawyer and investor who was based on the West Coast and had emerged as Buffett's confidant. By the early 1980s, Munger and Buffett would formalize their partnership at Berkshire with Munger becoming vice-chairman, a position he still holds.

. . .

Fear of inflation was a constant theme in Berkshire's annual reports throughout the 1970s and into the early 1980s. The conventional wisdom at the time was that hard assets (gold, timber, and the like) were the most effective inflation hedges. Buffett, however, under Munger's influence and in a shift from Graham's traditional approach, had come to a different conclusion. His contrarian insight was that companies with low capital needs and the ability to raise prices were actually best positioned to resist inflation's corrosive effects.

This led him to invest in consumer brands and media properties—businesses with "franchises," dominant market positions, or brand names. Along with this shift in investment criteria came an important shift to longer holding periods, which allowed for long-term pretax compounding of investment values.

It is hard to overstate the significance of this change. Buffet was switching at midcareer from a proven, lucrative investment approach that focused on the balance sheet and tangible assets, to an entirely different one that looked to the future and emphasized the income statement and hard-to-quantify assets like brand names and market share. To determine margin of safety, Buffett relied now on discounted cash flows and private market values instead of Graham's beloved net working capital calculation. It was not unlike Bob Dylan's controversial and roughly contemporaneous switch from acoustic to electric guitar.

This tectonic shift played itself out throughout the 1970s in Berkshire's insurance portfolios, which saw an increasing proportion of media and branded consumer products companies. By the end of the decade, this transition was complete, and Buffett's portfolio included outright ownership of See's Candies and the *Buffalo News* as well as large stock positions in the *Washington Post,* GEICO, and General Foods.

In the first half of the 1980s, Buffett focused on adding to the company's portfolio of wholly owned companies, buying the Nebraska Furniture Mart for $60 million in 1983 and Scott

## See's: The Turning Point

A pivotal investment in Buffett's shift in investment focus from "cigar butts" to "franchises" was the acquisition in 1972 of See's Candies. Buffett and Munger bought See's for $25 million. At the time, the company had $7 million in tangible book value and $4.2 million in pretax profits, so they were paying a seemingly exorbitant multiple of over three times book value (but only six times pretax income). See's was expensive by Graham's standards, and he would never have touched it. Buffett and Munger, however, saw a beloved brand with excellent returns on capital and untapped pricing power, and they immediately installed a new CEO, Chuck Huggins, to take advantage of this opportunity.

See's has experienced relatively little unit growth since it was acquired, but due to the power of its brand, it has been able to consistently raise prices, resulting in an extraordinary 32 percent compound return on Berkshire's investment over its first twenty-seven years. (After 1999, See's results were no longer reported separately.)

During the last thirty-nine years, the company has sent $1.65 *billion* in free cash to Omaha on an original investment of $25 million. This cash has been redeployed with great skill by Buffett, and See's has been a critical building block in Berkshire's success. (Interestingly, purchase price played a relatively minor role in generating these returns: had Buffett and Munger paid *twice* the price, the return would still have been a very attractive 21 percent.)

Fetzer, a conglomerate of niche industrial businesses, in 1985 for $315 million. In 1986, he made his largest investment yet, committing $500 million to help his friend Tom Murphy, the CEO of Capital Cities, acquire ABC. Buffett and Berkshire ended up owning 18 percent of the combined company, and it became the third of his "permanent" stock holdings, alongside GEICO and The Washington Post Company.

By 1987, in advance of the October market crash, Buffett had sold all of the stocks in his insurance company portfolios, except for his three core positions. After the Capital Cities transaction, he did not make another public market investment until 1989, when he announced that he had made the largest investment in Berkshire's history: investing an amount equal to *one-quarter* of Berkshire's book value in the Coca-Cola Company, purchasing 7 percent of its shares.

In the late 1980s, Buffett made a handful of investments in convertible preferred securities in publicly traded companies, including Salomon Brothers, Gillette, US Airways, and Champion Industries. The dividends from these securities were tax advantaged, providing Berkshire with an attractive yield and the potential for upside (via the ability to convert to common stock) if the companies performed well.

In 1991, Salomon Brothers was at the center of a major financial scandal, accused of fixing prices in government Treasury bill auctions, and Buffett was drafted as interim CEO to help the company navigate the crisis. He devoted himself full-time for a little over nine months to this project, calming regulators, installing a new CEO, and attempting to rationalize Salomon's byzantine compensation programs. In the end, the company ended up paying a relatively small settlement and eventually returned to its former prosperity. Late in 1996, Salomon was sold to Sandy Weill's Travelers Corporation for $9 billion, a significant premium to Buffett's investment cost.

In the early 1990s, Buffett continued to make selected, sizable public market investments, including large positions in Wells

Fargo (1990), General Dynamics (1992), and American Express (1994). As the decade progressed, Buffett once again shifted his focus to acquisitions, culminating in two significant insurance transactions: the $2.3 billion purchase in 1996 of the half of GEICO that he did not already own and the purchase of reinsurer General Re in 1998 for $22 billion in Berkshire stock, the largest transaction in the company's history.

In the late 1990s and early 2000s, Buffett was an opportunistic buyer of private companies, many of them in industries out of favor after the September 11 terrorist attacks, including Shaw Carpets, Benjamin Moore Paints, and Clayton Homes. He also made a series of significant investments in the electric utility industry through MidAmerican Energy, a joint venture with his Omaha friend Walter Scott, the former CEO of Kiewit Construction.

During this period, Buffett was also active in a variety of investing areas outside of traditional equity markets. In 2003, he made a large ($7 billion) and very lucrative bet on junk bonds, then enormously out of favor. In 2003 and 2004, he made a significant ($20 billion) currency bet against the dollar, and in 2006, he announced Berkshire's first international acquisition: the $5 billion purchase of Istar, a leading manufacturer of cutting tools and blades based in Israel that has prospered under Berkshire's ownership.

Several years of inactivity followed, interrupted by the financial crisis in the wake of the Lehman Brothers bankruptcy, after which Buffett entered one of the most active investing periods of his career. This stretch of activity reached its climax with Berkshire's purchase of the nation's largest railroad, the Burlington Northern Santa Fe, in early 2010 at a total valuation of $34.2 billion.

So, here are those interplanetary numbers. From June, 1965, when Buffett assumed control of Berkshire, through 2011, the value of the company's shares had increased at a phenomenal compound rate of *20.7 percent,* dwarfing the *9.3 percent* returns of the S&P 500 over the same period (see figure 8-1). A dollar invested at the time of Buffett's takeover was worth *$6,265* forty-five years later. (A dollar invested at the time of Buffett's first stock purchase was worth over $10,000.) That same dollar invested in the S&P was worth *$62.*

**FIGURE 8-1**

**Berkshire Hathaway value of $1**

*Source:* Center for Research in Security Prices (CRSP) and Compustat.

During Buffett's long tenure, Berkshire's returns have exceeded those of the S&P by an extraordinary *hundredfold,* massively out-performing GE in the Welch era and any index of peers.

## The Nuts and Bolts

Buffett's exceptional results derived from an idiosyncratic approach in three critical and interrelated areas: capital generation, capital allocation, and management of operations.

Charlie Munger has said that the secret to Berkshire's long-term success has been its ability to "generate funds at 3 percent and invest them at 13 percent," and this consistent ability to create low-cost funds for investment has been an underappreciated contributor to the company's financial success.[1] Remarkably, Buffett has almost entirely eschewed debt and equity issuances—virtually all of Berkshire's investment capital has been generated internally.

The company's primary source of capital has been float from its insurance subsidiaries, although very significant cash has also been provided by wholly owned subsidiaries and by the occasional sale of investments. Buffett has in effect created a capital "flywheel" at Berkshire, with funds from these sources being used to acquire full or partial interests in other cash-generating businesses whose earnings in turn fund other investments, and so on.

Insurance is Berkshire's most important business by a wide margin and the critical foundation of its extraordinary growth. Buffett developed a distinctive approach to the insurance business, which bears interesting similarities to his broader approach to management and capital allocation.

When Buffett acquired National Indemnity in 1967, he was among the first to recognize the leverage inherent in insurance companies with the ability to generate low-cost float. The acquisition was, in his words, a "watershed" for Berkshire. As he explains, "Float is money we hold but don't own. In an insurance operation, float arises because premiums are received before losses are paid, an interval that sometimes extends over many years. During that time, the insurer invests the money."[2] This is another example of a powerful iconoclastic metric, one that the rest of the industry largely ignored at the time.

Over time, Buffett evolved an idiosyncratic strategy for his insurance operations that emphasized profitable underwriting and float generation over growth in premium revenue. This approach, wildly different from most other insurance companies, relied on a willingness to avoid underwriting insurance when pricing was low, even if short-term profitability might suffer, and, conversely, a propensity to write extraordinarily large amounts of business when prices were attractive.

This approach led to lumpy, but highly profitable, underwriting results. As an example, in 1984, Berkshire's largest property and casualty (P&C) insurer, National Indemnity, wrote $62.2 million in premiums. Two years later, premium volumes grew an extraordinary *sixfold* to $366.2 million. By 1989, they had fallen back 73 percent to $98.4 million and did not return to the $100 million level for *twelve years*. Three years later, in 2004, the company wrote over $600 million in premiums. Over this period, National Indemnity averaged an annual underwriting profit of 6.5 percent as a percentage of premiums. In contrast, over the same period, the typical property and casualty insurer averaged a *loss* of 7 percent.

This sawtooth pattern of revenue (see figure 8-2) would be virtually impossible for an independent, publicly traded insurer

**FIGURE 8-2**

## Berkshire Hathaway premium growth has been much spikier than that of the industry overall

**Premiums written (index)**

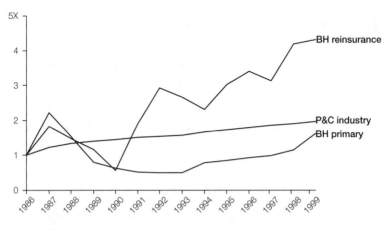

*Source:* P&C industry premium data is from Best's P&C Insurance Aggregates and Averages—total premiums written. Berkshire Hathaway data is from annual reports.

to explain to Wall Street. Because, however, Berkshire's insurance subsidiaries are part of a much larger diversified company, they are shielded from Wall Street scrutiny. This provides a major competitive advantage—allowing National Indemnity and Berkshire's other insurance businesses to focus on profitability, not premium growth. As Buffet has said, "Charlie and I have always preferred a lumpy 15 percent to a smooth 12 percent return."[3]

Float for all of Berkshire's insurance businesses grew enormously over this period, from $237 million in 1970 to over $70 *billion* in 2011. This incredibly low-cost source of funds has been the rocket fuel propelling Berkshire's phenomenal results, and, as we will see, these alternating periods of inactivity and decisive action mirror the pattern of Berkshire's investing activities. In both insurance and investing, Buffett believes the key to long-term success is "temperament," a willingness to be "fearful when others are greedy and greedy when they are fearful."[4]

The other important source of capital at Berkshire has been earnings from wholly owned companies. These earnings have become increasingly important over the last two decades as Buffett has added aggressively to Berkshire's portfolio of businesses. In 1990, pretax earnings from wholly owned operating companies were $102 million. In 2000, they were $918 million, a 24.5 percent compound growth rate. By 2011, they had reached an extraordinary $6.9 *billion*.

. . .

Now we'll turn our attention to how Buffett deploys the geyser of capital provided by Berkshire's operations. Whenever Buffett buys a company, he takes immediate control of the cash flow, insisting that excess cash be sent to Omaha for allocation. As Charlie Munger points out, "Unlike operations (which are very decentralized), capital allocation at Berkshire is highly centralized."[5] This mix of loose and tight, of delegation and hierarchy, was present at all the other outsider companies but generally not to Berkshire's extreme degree.

Buffett, already an extraordinarily successful investor, came to Berkshire uniquely prepared for allocating capital. Most CEOs are limited by prior experience to investment opportunities within their own industry—they are hedgehogs. Buffett, in contrast, by virtue of his prior experience evaluating investments in a wide variety of securities and industries, was a classic fox and had the advantage of choosing from a much wider menu of allocation options, including the purchase of private companies and publicly traded stocks. Simply put, the more investment options a CEO has, the more likely he or she is to make high-return decisions, and this broader palate has translated into a significant competitive advantage for Berkshire.

Buffett's approach to capital allocation was unique: he never paid a dividend or repurchased significant amounts of stock. Instead, with Berkshire's companies typically requiring little capital investment, he focused on investing in publicly traded stocks and acquiring private companies, options not available to most CEOs who lacked his extensive investment experience. Before we look at these two areas, however, let's first examine a critical early decision.

After a brief flirtation with the textile business, Buffett chose early on to make *no* further investments in Berkshire's low-return legacy suit-linings business and to harvest all excess capital and deploy it elsewhere. In contrast, Burlington Industries, the largest company in the textile business then and now, chose a different path, deploying all available capital into its existing business between 1965 and 1985. Over that twenty-year period, Burlington's stock appreciated at a paltry annual rate of 0.6 percent; Berkshire's compound return was a remarkable 27 percent. These differing results tell an important capital allocation parable: the value of being in businesses with attractive returns on capital, and the related importance of *getting out* of low-return businesses.

This was a key decision for Berkshire and makes a more general point. A critical part of capital allocation, one that receives less attention than more glamorous activities like acquisitions, is deciding which businesses are no longer deserving of future investment due to low returns. The outsider CEOs were generally ruthless in closing or selling businesses with poor future prospects and concentrating their capital on business units whose returns met their internal targets. As Buffett said when he finally closed Berkshire's textile business in 1985, "Should you find yourself in a chronically leaking boat, energy devoted to changing vessels is likely to be more productive than energy devoted to patching leaks."[6]

· · ·

Buffett is still best known for stock market investing, which was the primary channel for Berkshire's capital during his first twenty-five years as CEO. Buffett's public market returns are Ruthian by any measure, and there are several different ways to look at them. As we have seen, the average returns for the Buffett Partnership from 1957 to 1969 were *30.4 percent,* and according to a study in *Money Week* magazine, Berkshire's investment returns from 1985 through 2005 were an extraordinary *25 percent.*[7]

Because of its importance to Berkshire's overall returns and the window it provides on Buffett's broader capital allocation philosophy, it's worth taking a close look at one particular facet of Buffett's approach to public market investing: portfolio management. *Portfolio management*—how many stocks an investor owns and how long he holds them—has an enormous impact on returns. Two investors with the same investment philosophy but different approaches to portfolio management will produce dramatically different results. Buffett's approach to managing Berkshire's stock investments has been distinguished by two primary characteristics: a high degree of concentration and extremely long holding periods. In each of these areas, his thinking is unconventional.

Buffett believes that exceptional returns come from concentrated portfolios, that excellent investment ideas are rare, and he has repeatedly told students that their investing results would improve if at the beginning of their careers, they were handed a twenty-hole punch card representing the total number of investments they could make in their investing lifetimes. As he summarized in the 1993 annual report, "We believe that a policy of portfolio concentration may well decrease risk if it raises, as it should, both the intensity with which an investor thinks about a business and the comfort level he must feel with its economic characteristics before buying into it."[8]

Buffett's pattern of investment at Berkshire has been similar to the pattern of underwriting at his insurance subsidiaries, with long periods of inactivity interspersed with occasional large investments. The top five positions in Berkshire's portfolio have typically accounted for a remarkable 60–80 percent of total value. This compares with 10–20 percent for the typical mutual fund portfolio. On at least four occasions, Buffett invested over 15 percent of Berkshire's book value in a single stock, and he once had *40 percent* of the Buffett Partnership invested in American Express.

The other distinguishing characteristic of Buffett's approach to portfolio management is extraordinarily long holding periods. He has held his current top five stock positions (with the exception of IBM, which was purchased in 2011) for *over* twenty years on average. This compares with an average holding period of less than one year for the typical mutual fund. This translates into an exceptionally low level of investment activity, characterized by Buffett as "inactivity bordering on sloth."

These two portfolio management tenets combine to form a powerful and highly selective filter, one that very few companies pass through.

Interestingly, despite his historic advocacy of stock repurchases, Buffett (with the exception of a few small, early buybacks) is the only CEO in this book who did not buy back significant amounts of his company's stock. Despite admiring and encouraging the re-purchases of other CEOs, he has felt buybacks were counter to Berkshire's unique, partnership-like culture and could potentially tamper with the bonds of trust built up over many years of hon-est, forthright communications and outstanding returns.

That being said, Buffett is nothing if not opportunistic. On the rare occasions (two, actually) when Berkshire's stock traded for extended periods at valuations well below intrinsic value, Buffett broke with tradition and explored a repurchase—as he did in early 2001, when the stock fell precipitously during the Internet bubble, and, more recently, in September 2011, when he announced that he would buy back significant amounts of stock at prices below 1.1 times book value. In both cases, the stock quickly moved up, preventing Berkshire from purchasing a meaningful number of shares.

. . .

The other major outlet for Berkshire's capital has been the pur-chase of private companies. This channel has quietly become the primary one for Buffett over the last twenty years, culminating

## Two Interesting Patterns

For those interested in a deeper dive into Buffett's stock market investing, two other patterns are worthy of notice.

The first is a deep-rooted contrarianism. Buffett has frequently cited Benjamin Graham's "Mr. Market" analogy, in which "an obliging fellow named 'Mr. Market' shows up every day to either buy from you or sell to you . . . the more manic-depressive this chap is, the greater the opportunities available to the investor."[a] Buffett systematically buys when Graham's Mr. Market is feeling most blue. The majority of Berkshire's major public market investments originated in some sort of industry or company crisis that obscured the value of a strong underlying business.

The following table demonstrates this pattern.

| Company | Date of first investment | Contrarian context |
|---|---|---|
| American Express | 1964 | Salad oil scandal |
| Washington Post | 1973 | Government broadcast license challenge |
| GEICO | 1976 | Potential insolvency |
| Wells Fargo | 1989 | Southern California recession and real estate crisis |
| Freddie Mac | 1989 | Recession, S&L crisis |
| General Dynamics | 1992 | Post–Cold War defense industry slump |

| Company | Date of investment | Management/ strategic change |
| --- | --- | --- |
| GEICO | 1976 | Focus on core insurance business, new CEO, prior holding |
| General Foods | 1979 | Focus on core brands, new CEO, buybacks |
| Coca-Cola | 1988 | Divesting noncore businesses, buybacks, relatively new CEO |
| General Dynamics | 1992 | Divestitures, buybacks, new CEO |
| American Express | 1994 | Divesting Lehman, new CEO, prior holding |

The second pattern is timing investments to coincide with significant management or strategy changes. Buffett uses the analogy of a pro-am golf event to describe these investment opportunities, which arise when a company with an excellent "franchise-type" business invests in other businesses with lower returns: "Even if all of the amateurs are hopeless duffers, the team's best-ball score will be respectable because of the dominating skills of the professional."[b] When, however, Buffett sees that a new management team is removing the amateurs from the foursome and returning focus to the company's core businesses, he pays close attention, as the preceding table demonstrates.

a. Berkshire Hathaway annual reports, 1977–2011.

b. Berkshire Hathaway annual reports, 1989.

in the massive Burlington Northern purchase in early 2010. His approach to these acquisitions is homegrown and unique, and table 8-2 compares it with that of conventional private equity firms.

Buffett has created an attractive, highly differentiated option for sellers of large private businesses, one that falls somewhere between an IPO and a private equity sale. A sale to Berkshire is unique in allowing an owner/operator to achieve liquidity while continuing to run the company without interference or Wall Street scrutiny. Buffett offers an environment that is completely free of corporate bureaucracy, with unlimited access to capital for worthwhile projects. This package is highly differentiated from the private equity alternative, which promises a high level of investor involvement and a typical five-year holding period before the next exit event.

Buffett never participates in auctions. As David Sokol, the (now former) CEO of MidAmerican Energy and NetJets, told me, "We simply don't get swept away by the excitement of bidding."[9] Instead, remarkably, Buffett has created a system in which the owners of leading private companies *call him*. He avoids negotiating valuation, asking interested sellers to contact him and name their price. He promises to give an answer "usually in five minutes or less."[10] This requirement forces potential sellers to move quickly to their lowest acceptable price and ensures that his time is used efficiently.

Buffett does not spend significant time on traditional due diligence and arrives at deals with extraordinary speed, often within a few days of first contact. He never visits operating facilities and rarely meets with management before deciding on an acquisition.

TABLE 8-2

**Buffett's approach to private company acquisitions versus that of private equity firms**

|  | Buffett | PE firms |
|---|---|---|
| Holding period | "Forever" | ~ 5 years |
| Management | Existing CEO | New CEO (often) |
| Leverage | None | A lot |
| Deal source | Direct | Auction |
| Postacquisition management interaction | Infrequent | Frequent |
| Cost cutting | Never | Usually |
| Due diligence | Cursory | Extensive |
| Use of outside advisers | Never | Always |
| Compensation system | Simple | Complex |

Tom Murphy told me, "Capital Cities was one of the biggest investments Berkshire had ever made. . . . It took only fifteen minutes to talk through the deal and agree on terms."[11]

Buffett, the master delegator, has never, however, delegated capital allocation decisions. There is no business development team or investment committee at Berkshire, and Buffett never relies on investment bankers, accountants, or lawyers (with the exception of Munger) for advice. He does his own analytical work and handles all negotiations personally. He never looks at the forecasts provided by intermediaries, preferring instead to focus on historical financial statements and make his own projections. He is able to move quickly because he only buys companies in industries he knows well, allowing him to focus quickly on key operating metrics. As Charlie Munger has said about Berkshire's approach to acquisitions, "We don't try to do acquisitions, we wait for no-brainers."[12]

. . .

Buffett, in addition to being the greatest investor of his generation, has proven to be an extremely effective manager of Berkshire's growing, polyglot portfolio of operating businesses. Over the last ten years, Berkshire has grown earnings per share significantly, and despite its size and diversity, the company operates with extraordinary efficiency—consistently ranking in the top quartile of the *Fortune* 500 for return on tangible assets.

So, how does Buffett achieve these operating results? Beneath his avuncular exterior, Buffett is a deeply unconventional CEO, which is perhaps best seen by comparing his approach with that of Jack Welch (see table 8-3), who thrived at GE with a system that emphasized centralized strategic initiatives (Six Sigma, and so on), rotating CEOs, and a frenetic pace of travel and meetings. The contrast in management styles could hardly be more dramatic (although Buffett has deep admiration for Welch's abilities).

Buffett came to the CEO role without *any* relevant operating experience and consciously designed Berkshire to allow him to focus his time on capital allocation, while spending as little time as possible managing operations, where he felt he could add little value. As a result, the touchstone of the Berkshire system is extreme decentralization. If Teledyne, Capital Cities, and the other companies in this book had decentralized management styles and philosophies, Berkshire's is positively anarchic by comparison.

**TABLE 8-3**

## Comparison of Welch's and Buffett's approaches to management

|  | Welch | Buffett |
|---|---|---|
| Earnings pattern | Smooth | Lumpy |
| Employees | 400,000 | 270,000 |
| Headquarters staff | Thousands | 23 |
| Travel | Lots | Little |
| Primary activity | Meetings | Reading |
| Investor relations time | A lot | None |
| Tone of workday | Frenetic/busy | Quiet/unscheduled |
| Change managers | A lot | Almost never |
| Off-site meetings | Frequently | Never |
| Strategic planning | Regularly | Never |
| Stock splits | Yes | No |

In a company with over 270,000 employees, there are only 23 at corporate headquarters in Omaha. There are *no* regular budget meetings for Berkshire companies. The CEOs who run Berkshire's subsidiary companies simply never hear from Buffett unless they call for advice or seek capital for their businesses. He summarizes this approach to management as "hire well, manage little" and believes this extreme form of decentralization increases the overall efficiency of the organization by reducing overhead and releasing entrepreneurial energy.[13]

. . .

In his 1986 Berkshire annual report, Buffett (as we saw in the introduction) described the discovery of the surprisingly powerful *institutional imperative,* which led managers to mindlessly imitate their peers. Cognizant of Churchill's quotation (which he has frequently cited), he has intentionally structured his company and life to avoid the effects of this imperative. Buffett spends his time differently than other *Fortune* 500 CEOs, managing his schedule to avoid unnecessary distractions and preserving *uninterrupted* time to read (five newspapers daily and countless annual reports) and think. He prides himself on keeping a blank calendar, devoid of regular meetings. He does not have a computer in his office and has never had a stock ticker.

Buffett's approach to investor relations is also unique and homegrown. Buffett estimates the average CEO spends 20 percent of his time communicating with Wall Street. In contrast, he spends no time with analysts, never attends investment conferences, and has never provided quarterly earnings guidance. He prefers to communicate with his investors through detailed annual reports and meetings, both of which are unique.

Printed on plain, uncoated paper with a simple, single-color cover, Berkshire's annual report *looks* different from other annual reports. The core of the report is a long essay written by Buffett (with editorial assistance from Carol Loomis) that provides a detailed review of the company's various businesses over the past year. The style is direct and informal, and the reports are models of concision and clarity, with detailed information for each operating division and an "owner's manual" clearly outlining Buffett and Munger's distinctive operating philosophy.

The annual meetings are also unique. The administrative portion of the meeting typically takes no more than fifteen minutes, after which Buffett and Munger answer questions from shareholders for up to five hours. The meetings attract enormous crowds (over thirty-five thousand people attended the 2011 meeting), and Buffett has taken to referring to them as "the Woodstock of capitalism."[14] The annual reports and meetings reinforce a powerful culture that values frugality, independent thinking, and long-term stewardship. (Also, whimsy and humor—when Buffett stepped out of character in the early 1990s and purchased a corporate plane, he dubbed it "The Indefensible" and disclosed it in the annual report in laughably small print.)

Another unconventional shareholder practice relates to stock splits. Buffett has famously eschewed splitting Berkshire's A shares, which currently trade at over $120,000, more than fifty times the price of the next-highest issue on the New York Stock Exchange (NYSE). He believes these splits are purely cosmetic and likens the process to dividing a pizza into eight versus four slices, with no change in calories or asset value delivered. Avoiding stock splits is yet another filter, helping Berkshire to self-select for long-term owners. In 1996, he reluctantly agreed to create a lower-priced class of B shares, which traded at one-thirtieth of the A shares and were the second-highest-priced issue on the NYSE. (In connection with the Burlington Northern deal in early 2010, Buffett agreed to split the B shares a further 50:1 to accommodate the railroad's smaller investors.)

. . .

All of this adds up to something much more powerful than a business or investment strategy. Buffett has developed a *worldview* that at its core emphasizes the development of long-term relationships with excellent people and businesses and the avoidance

## Buffett and Sarbanes-Oxley

Buffett's approach to corporate governance is also unconventional, contradicting many of the dictates of the Sarbanes-Oxley legislation. Buffett believes that the best boards are composed of relatively small groups (Berkshire has twelve directors) of experienced businesspeople with large ownership stakes. (He requires that all directors have significant personal capital invested in Berkshire's stock.) He believes directors should have exposure to the consequences of poor decisions (Berkshire does not carry insurance for its directors) and should not be reliant on the income from board fees, which are minimal at Berkshire.

This approach, which leaves him with a small group of "insiders" by Sarbanes-Oxley standards, provides a stark contrast with most public company boards, whose members rarely have meaningful personal capital invested alongside shareholders, whose downsides are limited by insurance, and whose fees often represent a high percentage of their total income. Which approach leads to better alignment with shareholders?

---

of unnecessary turnover, which can interrupt the powerful chain of economic compounding that is the essence of long-term value creation.

In fact, Buffett can perhaps best be understood as a manager/investor/philosopher whose primary objective is turnover reduction. Berkshire's many iconoclastic policies all share the objective of selecting for the best people and businesses and reducing the significant financial and human costs of churn, whether of managers, investors, or shareholders. To Buffett and Munger, there is a compelling, Zen-like logic in choosing to associate with the best and in avoiding unnecessary change. Not only is it a path to exceptional economic returns, it is a more balanced way to lead a life; and among the many lessons they have to teach, the power of these long-term relationships may be the most important.

# Radical Rationality

## The Outsider's Mind-Set

You are right not because others agree with you, but because your facts and reasoning are sound.

—*Benjamin Graham*

What makes him a leader is precisely that he is able to think things through for himself.

—*William Deresiewicz, lecture to West Point plebe class,
   October 2009*

Stepping back, we can see in figure 9-1 the value of a dollar invested with the outsider CEOs versus their peers, the broader market, and Jack Welch.

Pretty impressive—the numbers speak for themselves and nicely summarize the achievement of these extraordinary executives. These phenomenal records, however, were assembled

FIGURE 9-1

## Value of $1

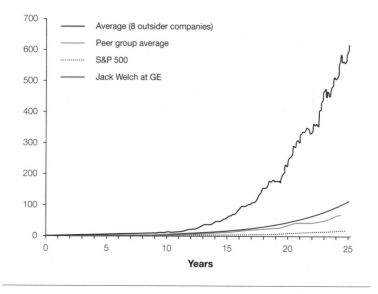

for the most part last century. So the question is, are the experiences and lessons of these CEOs still relevant to managers and investors operating in today's rapidly changing competitive environment? The answer is borne out in the examples of two more recent companies: one small (Pre-Paid Legal) and one large (ExxonMobil).

Pre-Paid Legal Services was until recently a publicly traded company that sold legal plans to individuals and businesses. These plans are effectively insurance products—in return for an annual premium, customers are covered for expenses that might arise from a wide range of potential legal activities, including litigation, real estate, trusts, and wills. These plans were invented in the 1970s, and Pre-Paid Legal grew rapidly throughout the 1980s and 1990s. What's interesting about the company is that after this strong initial growth, its revenues have been virtually flat over the last ten years.

This pattern of rapid growth followed by a sudden and extended flattening in results has historically been a recipe for horrific stock market returns. Over that same period of time, however, Pre-Paid's stock appreciated *fourfold,* dramatically outperforming both the market and its industry peers. How did the company achieve these results? Starting in late 1999, its CEO, Harland Stonecipher, realized that his market was maturing and that additional investments in growth were unlikely to have attractive returns. At the urging of his board (which, unusually for a public company, included several large investors), he began a systematic and aggressive program of optimizing free cash flow and systematically returning capital to shareholders through an aggressive stock repurchase program. Over the next twelve years, Stonecipher bought in over 50 percent of shares outstanding, to the sustained applause of his shareholders and the stock market, and in June 2011, agreed to sell his company to a private equity firm for a significant premium.

Since Pre-Paid Legal is a smaller, closely held company, it's important to look for another example among larger firms. A big one—a *really* big one—is ExxonMobil, the world's largest company by market capitalization. Since 1977, Exxon (and later ExxonMobil) has generated a phenomenal *15 percent* compound return for its investors, dwarfing both the market and its peers, a truly remarkable record given its size. When we look at how its managers achieved these results, the similarities with the outsider CEOs are striking. A handful of lessons stand out.

*Always Do the Math*

The outsider CEOs always started by asking what the return was. Every investment project generates a return, and the math is really just fifth-grade arithmetic, but these CEOs did it consistently, used conservative assumptions, and only went forward with projects that offered compelling returns. They focused on the key assumptions, did not believe in overly detailed spreadsheets, and performed the analysis themselves, not relying on subordinates or advisers. The outsider CEOs believed that the value of financial projections was determined by the quality of the assumptions, *not* by the number of pages in the presentation, and many developed succinct, single-page analytical templates that focused employees on key variables.

In Daniel Kahneman's excellent recent book, *Thinking, Fast and Slow,* he lays out a model for human decision making that evolved from his thirty years of Nobel Prize–winning research.[1] Kahneman's paradigm features two distinct systems. System 1 is the purely instinctive pattern recognition mode that is instantly engaged in any situation and arrives at decisions very quickly using rules of thumb. System 2 is the slower, more reflective track that employs more complex analysis. System 2 can override system 1. The problem is that it takes more time and effort to engage system 2, and for that reason, it is underutilized in many of us.

According to Kahneman, the key to using system 2 is often a catalyst or trigger, and for the outsider CEOs, these deceptively simple, "one-pager" analyses often served that function. They ensured a focus on empirical data and prevented blind crowd following. As such, they were inoculations against conventional wisdom, and they spread widely throughout the outsider companies. As George Roberts, Henry Singleton's COO at Teledyne, told *Forbes* magazine, "Capital discipline is so ingrained in our managers that very few low-returning proposals are ever presented to us."[2]

Under the leadership of CEO Rex Tillerson and his curmudgeonly predecessor, Lee Raymond, ExxonMobil has exhibited similar discipline, requiring a minimum 20 percent return on all capital projects. During the recent financial crisis, as energy prices fell, Tillerson and his team were criticized by Wall Street analysts for lowering production levels. They simply refused, however, to pump additional oil from projects with insufficient returns, even if it meant lower near-term profits.

## The Denominator Matters

These CEOs shared an intense focus on maximizing *value per share*. To do this, they didn't simply focus on the numerator, total company value, which can be grown by any number of means, including overpaying for acquisitions or funding internal capital projects that don't make economic sense. They also focused intently on managing the denominator through the careful financing of investment projects and opportunistic share repurchases. These repurchases were not made to prop up stock prices or to offset option grants (two popular rationales for buybacks today) but rather because they offered attractive returns as investments in their own right.

Alone among the major energy companies, ExxonMobil has been an aggressive purchaser of its own stock, buying in over 25 percent of shares outstanding in the last five years. In the teeth of the post-Lehman meltdown, the company actually accelerated its repurchases.

## A Feisty Independence

The outsider CEOs were master delegators, running highly decentralized organizations and pushing operating decisions down to the lowest, most local levels in their organizations. They did not, however, delegate capital allocation decisions. As Charlie Munger described it to me, their companies were "an odd blend of decentralized operations and highly centralized capital allocation," and this mix of loose and tight, of delegation and hierarchy, proved to be a very powerful counter to the institutional imperative.[3]

In addition to thinking independently, they were comfortable acting with a minimum of input from outside advisers. There is something out of *High Noon* in John Malone showing up solo to face a phalanx of AT&T corporate development staff, lawyers, and accountants; or Bill Stiritz showing up alone with a yellow legal pad for due diligence on a potential multibillion-dollar transaction; or Warren Buffett making a decision on a potential acquisition for Berkshire in a single day without ever visiting the company.

## Charisma Is Overrated

The outsider CEOs were also distinctly unpromotional and spent considerably less time on investor relations than their peers. They did not offer earnings guidance or participate in Wall Street conferences. As a group, they were not extroverted or overly charismatic. In this regard, they had the quality of humility that Jim

Collins emphasized in his excellent *Good to Great*. They did not seek (or usually attract) the spotlight. Their returns, however, more than compensated for this introversion.

Tillerson is involved in all major capital allocation decisions at ExxonMobil. He rarely participates on earnings calls or goes to conferences and is known among the Wall Street analyst community for his laconic communication style.

### A Crocodile-Like Temperament That Mixes Patience . . .

Armed with their return calculations, all (with the notable exception of John Malone, who was constantly buying cable companies in pursuit of scale) were willing to wait long periods of time (in the case of Dick Smith at General Cinema, an entire decade) for the right opportunity to emerge. Like Katharine Graham, many of them created enormous shareholder value by simply avoiding overpriced "strategic" acquisitions, staying on the sidelines during periods of acquisition feeding frenzy.

Until recently, ExxonMobil hadn't closed a significant purchase in over ten years.

### . . . With Occasional Bold Action

Interestingly, as we've seen, this penchant for empiricism and analysis did not result in timidity. Just the opposite, actually: on the rare occasions when they found projects with compelling returns, they could act with boldness and blinding speed. Each made at least one acquisition or investment that equaled 25 percent or more of their firm's enterprise value. Tom Murphy made one (ABC) that was greater than his entire company's value. In 1999 (at a time when oil prices were at historic lows), Exxon bought rival Mobil Corporation in a blockbuster transaction that totaled more than 50 percent of its enterprise value.

*The Consistent Application of a Rational, Analytical Approach to Decisions Large and Small*

These executives were capital surgeons, consistently directing available capital toward the most efficient, highest-returning projects. Over long periods of time, this discipline had an enormous impact on shareholder value through the steady accretion of value-enhancing decisions and (equally important) the avoidance of value-destroying ones. *This unorthodox mind-set, in itself, proved to be a substantial and sustainable competitive advantage for their companies.* It provided the equivalent of polarized lenses, allowing the outsider CEOs to cut through the glare of peer activity and conventional wisdom to see the core economic reality and make decisions accordingly.

There are numerous examples sprinkled throughout the book of the crispness and efficiency that resulted from this pragmatic analytical approach. These CEOs knew precisely what they were looking for, and so did their employees. They didn't overanalyze or overmodel, and they didn't look to outside consultants or bankers to confirm their thinking—they pounced. As Pat Mulcahy, Bill Stiritz's longtime lieutenant at Ralston Purina, put it, "We knew what we needed to focus on. Simple as that."[4]

In a 2009 article, *Barron's* described ExxonMobil's "distinctive" corporate culture with its "relentless focus on returns at the expense of ego."[5] Not coincidentally, this frugal culture produced exceptional results, and ExxonMobil has consistently led the oil and gas industry in return on equity over the last quarter century.

## A Prediction

Today, the combination of record corporate cash levels and generally low interest rates and P/E ratios presents a historic opportunity for aggressive capital allocation. This situation is particularly pronounced among the largest, bluest-chip technology businesses—companies like Cisco, Microsoft, and Dell—many of which are still run by members of their founding management teams, have enormous cash balances, and trade at unprecedented single-digit P/E multiples. I think it's likely one of these firms will reverse its historic emphasis on R&D investment and move to optimize returns through a combination of dramatically increased buybacks or dividends. Were this to happen, the market's response would likely be rapturous, and one can imagine Henry Singleton as the CEO of one of these companies, rubbing his hands together in delight at the opportunities.

### A Long-Term Perspective

Although frugal by nature, the outsider CEOs were also willing to invest in their businesses to build long-term value. To do this, they needed to ignore the quarterly earnings treadmill and tune out Wall Street analysts and the cacophony of cable shows like *Squawk Box* and *Mad Money,* with their relentless emphasis on short-term thinking. When Tom Murphy insisted on a huge spike in capital expenditures for a new printing plant or when John Malone bought expensive cutting-edge cable boxes in the late 1990s, they were consciously penalizing short-term earnings to improve their customers' experiences and defend long-term competitive positions.

This long-range perspective often leads to contrarian behavior. In contrast to its controversial decision to reduce production, ExxonMobil, alone among the major energy companies, resolutely maintained its spending on exploration during the financial crisis with a view toward optimizing long-term value. When other large players retrenched from the Canadian oil sands after energy prices plunged in early 2009, ExxonMobil moved forward with a large exploration project in Alberta even though it would penalize near-term earnings.

. . .

A high-profile contrast to Stonecipher and Tillerson's achievements is provided by the nation's largest financial institution, Citigroup, whose CEO, Chuck Prince, at the height of the mortgage and leverage tsunami of the mid-2000s, famously declared, "As long as the music is playing, you've got to get up and dance."[6] Prince was transfixed by the lure of conventional wisdom, by the institutional imperative, and he and his shareholders would soon dance off the cliff as the company's stock plunged from a 2007 high of $40 to less than $3 in early 2009. During a period of horrendous market and industry performance, Prince managed to underperform both the S&P and his peers.

What separated these CEOs (and the performance of their companies) was two distinctly different mind-sets. The outsider CEOs, like Stonecipher and Tillerson, tended to dance when everyone else was on the sidelines and to cling shyly to the periphery when the music was loudest. They were intelligent contrarians willing to lean against the wall indefinitely when returns were uninteresting.

In widely varying industries and market conditions, this group independently coalesced around a remarkably similar set of core principles. Fundamentally, Stonecipher, Tillerson, and their fellow outsider CEOs achieved extraordinary relative results by consistently zigging while their peers zagged; and as table 9-1 shows, in their zigging, they followed a virtually identical blueprint: *they disdained dividends, made disciplined (occasionally large) acquisitions, used leverage selectively, bought back a lot of stock, minimized taxes, ran decentralized organizations, and focused on cash flow over reported net income.*

Again, what matters is how you play the hand you're dealt, and these executives were dealt very different hands. Their circumstances varied widely—those facing Bill Anders after the fall of the Berlin Wall could not have been more different from those facing John Malone when he took over TCI during the cable television boom of the early 1970s. The key is optimizing within given circumstances. An analogy can be made to a high school football coach who every year has to adapt his strategy to the changing mix of players on his team (i.e., with a weak quarterback, he must run the ball), or to the head of a repertory theater company who must choose plays that fit her actors' unique mix of talents.

There is no strict formula here, no hard-and-fast rules—it does *not* always make sense to repurchase your own stock or to make acquisitions or to sit on the sidelines. The right capital allocation decision varies depending on the situation at any given point in time. This is why Henry Singleton believed flexibility was so essential. As a group, these CEOs faced the inherent uncertainty of the business world with a patient, rational, pragmatic opportunism, not a detailed set of strategic plans.

**TABLE 9-1**

## A shared worldview

| | First-time CEO | Dividends | Buyback 30%+ | Acquisitions 25%+ of market cap | Decentralized organizational structure | Wall Street guidance | Idiosyncratic metric | Tax focus |
|---|---|---|---|---|---|---|---|---|
| Henry Singleton | √ | No | √ | √ | √ | No | Teledyne return | High |
| Warren Buffett | √ | No | — | √ | √ | No | Float | Medium/high |
| Tom Murphy | √ | Low | √ | √ | √ | No | Cash flow margins | Medium/high |
| John Malone | √ | No | √ | √ | √ | No | EBITDA | High |
| Dick Smith | √ | Low | √ | √ | √ | No | Cash earnings | High |
| Bill Anders | √ | Low/special | √ | √ | √ | No | Cash ROI | High |
| Bill Stiritz | √ | Low | √ | √ | √ | No | IRR | High |
| Katharine Graham | √ | Low | √ | √ | √ | No | Cash IRR | Medium/high |

Their specific actions stemmed from a broader, shared mind-set and added up to nothing less than a new model for CEO success, one centered on the optimal management of firm resources. Although the outsider CEOs were an extraordinarily talented group, their advantage relative to their peers was one of *temperament,* not intellect. Fundamentally, they believed that what mattered was clear-eyed decision making, and in their cultures they emphasized the seemingly old-fashioned virtues of frugality and patience, independence and (occasional) boldness, rationality and logic.

Their unorthodox approach proved a robust source of competitive advantage across a wide variety of industries and mar-

TABLE 9-2

## A profile in iconoclasm

|  | Outsider CEOs | Peer CEOs |
|---|---|---|
| Experience | First-time CEOs with little prior managerial experience | Experienced managers with Gladwell's 10,000 hours |
| Primary activity | Capital allocation | Operations management and external communication |
| Objective | Optimize long-term value per share | Growth |
| Key metrics | Margins, returns, free cash flow | Revenues, reported net income |
| Personal qualities | Analytical, frugal, independent | Charismatic, extroverted |
| Orientation | Long-term | Short-term |
| Furry animal | Fox | Hedgehog |

ket conditions. Fundamentally, as table 9-2 demonstrates, these executives practiced a sort of radical rationality. They had the perspective of the long-term investor or owner, not the high-paid employee—a very different hat than most CEOs wear to work.

. . .

So, back to the question at hand: for whom are the experiences and lessons of these CEOs relevant? The short answer is virtually *any* manager or business owner. The good news is that you don't need to be a marketing or technical genius or a charismatic visionary to be a highly effective CEO. You do, however, need to understand capital allocation and to think carefully about how to best deploy your company's resources to create value for shareholders. You have to be willing to always ask what the return is and to go forward only with projects that offer attractive returns using conservative assumptions. And you have to have the confidence to occasionally do things differently from your peers. Managers and entrepreneurs who follow these principles, who commit to rationality and to thinking for themselves, can expect to make the most of the cards they're dealt and to delight their shareholders.

## Postlude: Old Dogs, Old Tricks

*If you can keep your head when all about you are losing theirs . . .*

—*Rudyard Kipling, "If"*

As the Nobel Prize–winning chemist Louis Pasteur once observed, "Chance favors . . . the prepared mind," and speaking of prepared minds, let's conclude by looking at how the two remaining active outsider CEOs, Warren Buffett and John Malone, navigated the financial meltdown that followed the September 2008 collapse of Lehman Brothers.

As you would expect, both pursued dramatically different courses from their peers'. At a time when virtually all of corporate America was sitting on the sidelines, shepherding cash, and nursing ailing balance sheets, these two lions in winter were actively on the prowl.

Buffett, after a long period of relative inactivity stretching back to the immediate aftermath of 9/11, has had one of the most active periods of his long career. Since the fourth quarter of 2008, he has deployed over *$80 billion* (over $15 billion of it in the first *twenty-five days* after the Lehman collapse) in a wide variety of investing activities:

- Purchased $8 billion of convertible preferred stock from Goldman Sachs and General Electric

- Made a number of common stock purchases (including Constellation Energy): $9 billion

- Provided mezzanine financing to Mars/Wrigley ($6.5 billion) and Dow Chemical ($3 billion)

- Bought various distressed debt securities in the open market: $8.9 billion

(*continued*)

- In Berkshire's largest deal ever by dollar value, bought the 77.5 percent of Burlington Northern that he didn't already own for $26.5 billion

- Acquired Lubrizol, a leading, publicly traded lubricant company for $8.7 billion

- Announced a sizable ($10.9 billion) new investment in IBM stock

Over the same period, John Malone has been quietly conducting an extended experiment in aggressive capital allocation across the disparate entities that were spun out of TCI's original programming arm, Liberty Media. In the depths of the financial crisis, Malone:

- Implemented a "leveraged equity growth" strategy at satellite programming giant DIRECTV—increasing debt and aggressively repurchasing stock (over 40 percent of shares outstanding in the last twenty-four months).

- Initiated a series of moves across the former Liberty entities, including the spin-off of cable programmer Starz/Encore and a debt-for-equity swap between Liberty Capital (owner of Malone's polyglot collection of public and private assets) and Liberty Interactive (home of the QVC shopping network and other online entities).

- Swept in and bought control of Sirius Broadcasting, the satellite radio service, through Liberty Capital, in a distressed (and extremely attractive) transaction at the nadir of the market in early 2009. He also bought back 11 percent of Liberty Capital's shares in the second quarter of 2010.

- Through his international cable arm, Liberty Global, announced the company's largest acquisition ever, the purchase
  of German cable company Unitymedia for over €5 billion
  (less than seven times cash flow), as well as the sale of its
  sizable stake in Japan's largest cable business for over nine
  times cash flow (with all proceeds sheltered from taxes by the
  company's enormous pool of net operating losses). He also
  continued Liberty Global's aggressive buyback program (the
  company has repurchased over *half* its shares in the last five
  years).

Phew . . . so while corporate America generally stood frozen on
the sidelines, these two wily CEOs engaged in an orgy of Keynesian
"animal spirits." They were, to qualify Buffett's dictum, *very* greedy
at a time when their peers trembled with unprecedented fear.

# Epilogue

*An Example and a Checklist*

Let's conclude with an example that shows the outsider approach at work in a different setting.

Suppose you own a successful high-end bakery, specializing in baguettes and fresh pastries. The key to your success is a special oven manufactured in Italy, and you have the high-class problem of more demand than you can keep up with.

You are faced with two choices for growing the business: expand into the space next door and buy a second oven, or open a new store, in a different part of town, which also requires a new oven. A competitor of yours in a different part of the city has recently expanded its store with great success, and you've recently read about a publicly traded baking company that has grown through carefully enlarging existing stores. Conventional wisdom points to expanding your store as the right path, but you sit down and do the math.

You start by calculating the up-front cost and likely revenues and profits for each scenario, using what you believe to be conservative assumptions. You then calculate the return for each, starting with the expansion option.

You've decided your personal hurdle rate: you will go forward only if the project can produce at least a 20 percent return. You make the following calculations: a new oven costs $50,000; additional space in your existing building costs $50,000 to build out and would likely produce incremental annual profits of $20,000 after labor, material, and other operating costs. So, you have $100,000 in up-front costs (the oven plus the build-out) and an expected annual profit of $20,000, for an expected return of 20 percent—right at your hurdle rate.

You then turn your attention to the new-store option. The up-front costs include an oven at a cost of $50,000 and $150,000 in build-out expenses. The scenarios for the new store are harder to predict (it's in a different part of town, and so on), but you assess the potential annual profit at $50,000–$75,000. So you calculate that you would spend $200,000 up front, and you would expect a return of 25–37.5 percent. This return, even at the lower end of the range, is clearly higher than the adjacent-space option; but before deciding which path to take, you ask yourself some important, qualitative questions:

- The new store is in a different part of town, and there is greater risk that sales will be different than what you forecast—how comfortable are you with your estimates?

- Is the higher return enough to compensate for this additional uncertainty?

- The new store requires twice the investment of the expansion option. Can you raise the extra $100,000 for the new-store option (and if so, at what cost)?

- Conversely, are there hidden benefits to the new store? Does it, for instance, diversify your operations, so that if sales decline in your existing store, you have some protection?

- Does opening a second store give you insight that allows you potentially to build a much larger company over time?

These are the sorts of capital allocation questions and decisions that managers and entrepreneurs have to wrestle with every day, regardless of the size of the enterprise (although larger companies will often hire consultants and investment bankers to help them with the answers), and the same methodical, analytically oriented thought process is essential to both the baker and the *Fortune* 500 CEO in making effective decisions.

This outsider approach, whether in a local business or a large corporate boardroom, doesn't seem that complicated; so why don't more people follow it? The answer is that it's harder than it looks. It's not easy to diverge from your peers, to ignore the institutional imperative, and in many ways the business world is like a high school cafeteria clouded by peer pressure. Particularly during times of crisis, the natural, instinctive reaction is to engage in what behaviorists call *social proof* and do what your peers are doing. In today's world of social media, instant messaging, and cacophonous cable shows, it's increasingly hard to cut through the noise, to step back and engage Kahneman's system 2, which is where a tool that's been much in the news lately can come in handy.

## The Outsider's Checklist

Checklists have proved to be extremely effective decision-making tools in fields as diverse as aviation, medicine, and construction. Their apparent simplicity belies their power, and thanks to Atul Gawande's excellent recent book, *The Checklist Manifesto*, their use is a hot topic these days.[1] Checklists are a particularly effective form of "choice architecture," working to promote analysis and rationality and eliminate the distractions that often cloud complex decisions. They are a systematic way to engage system [2], and for CEOs, they can be highly effective vaccines, inoculating against conventional wisdom and the institutional imperative.

Gawande advises that these lists are best kept to ten items or fewer, and we will conclude with a checklist drawn from the experiences of these outsider CEOs, to aid in making effective resource allocation decisions (and hopefully avoiding value-destroying ones).

So, here we go:

1. The allocation process should be CEO led, not delegated to finance or business development personnel.

2. Start by determining the *hurdle rate*—the minimum acceptable return for investment projects (one of the most important decisions any CEO makes).

> *Comment:* Hurdle rates should be determined in reference to the set of opportunities available to the com-

pany, and should generally exceed the blended cost
of equity and debt capital (usually in the midteens or
higher).

3. Calculate returns for all internal and external investment
alternatives, and rank them by return and risk (calculations do not need to be perfectly precise). Use conservative assumptions.

> *Comment:* Projects with higher risk (such as acquisi-
> tions) should require higher returns. Be very wary of
> the adjective *strategic*—it is often corporate code for
> *low returns*.

4. Calculate the return for stock repurchases. Require
that acquisition returns meaningfully exceed this
benchmark.

> *Comment:* While stock buybacks were a significant
> source of value creation for these outsider CEOs, they
> are not a panacea. Repurchases can also destroy value
> if they are made at exorbitant prices.

5. Focus on after-tax returns, and run all transactions by tax
counsel.

6. Determine acceptable, conservative cash and debt levels,
and run the company to stay within them.

7. Consider a decentralized organizational model. (What
is the ratio of people at corporate headquarters to
total employees—how does this compare to your peer
group?)

8. Retain capital in the business only if you have confidence you can generate returns over time that are above your hurdle rate.

9. If you do not have potential high-return investment projects, consider paying a dividend. Be aware, however, that dividend decisions can be hard to reverse and that dividends can be tax inefficient.

10. When prices are extremely high, it's OK to consider selling businesses or stock. It's also OK to close under-performing business units if they are no longer capable of generating acceptable returns.

Whether you are looking back or looking forward, the outsider approach to resource allocation offers a proven method for navigating the unpredictable, untidy world of business, one that has generated exceptional results across a wide variety of industries and market conditions. This checklist is a tool that can help any business, from the neighborhood bakery to the multinational conglomerate, adopt this proven approach and embrace the inherent uncertainty of the business world with open arms . . . and fresh eyes.

# Acknowledgments

*The Outsiders* originated while I was on vacation with my family in 2003. I work in a private equity firm and had been preparing for an upcoming talk at my firm's biannual CEO conference. The idea had been to profile an exceptional chief executive and share the lessons from that individual's career with the managers of our portfolio companies. I had chosen Henry Singleton and, in beginning the research process, had the good luck to find my way into a very talented network of second-year students at Harvard Business School, starting with Aleem Choudhry. Aleem, who was a Phi Beta Kappa graduate in physics from Stanford (where he had also played varsity tennis), did an excellent job on the project, and this collaboration created the research template for all the work that followed. At the end of the project, Aleem introduced me to another exceptional student, John Gilligan, then ending his first year at HBS. John, another Phi Beta, this time in chemistry from Harvard, agreed to do a similar independent study on Capital Cities, and we were off to the races.

Working with these students, I analyzed each of these CEOs and their peers in detail. Each project took a full academic year to complete and followed an identical process and timetable. The first semester was devoted to detailed analysis of historical financial reports for the companies and their peers (in total, we looked at over 1,000 company-years of financial data) and an in-depth review of other sources (including articles, books, and videos). The second semester focused on extensive interviews with former company executives, investors, Wall Street analysts, bankers, peer company executives, and, of course, the CEOs themselves (we spoke to every living CEO). These interviews often required extensive detective work to locate long-lost colleagues and investors, and, in total, we conducted over 100 of them.

So now, I have a lot of thanking to do, and I need to start by thanking that extremely talented collection of HBS students whom I had the great fortune to collaborate with on this project over the last eight years. This gifted group included Paul Buser (Ralston Purina), Aleem Choudhry (Teledyne), Erin Eisenberg (Berkshire Hathaway), Matt Estep (General Dynamics), John Gilligan (Capital Cities Broadcasting), Brian Hersman, Moritz Jobke (Tele-Communications Inc.), Christina Miller (The Washington Post Company), and Konstantinos Papakonstantinou (General Cinema).

Also from HBS, I'd like to thank professors Nabil El-Hage and Mike Roberts for their support, and a current student, Matt Klitus, who provided important analytical assistance as the manuscript was in its final stages.

I'd also like to thank those who offered to read the manuscript for their time and insight, including Bill Carey, Art Charpentier, Will Gardner, Giles Goodhead (a particularly close read), Irv Grousbeck, Bob Grusky, Mike Jackson, Chris Kimball, Sam MacAusland, Joe Niehaus, Brandon Nixon, David Simmons, Kevin Taweel, Lanny Thorndike, Tom Tryforos, Eliot Wadsworth, Ramsey Walker, and Steve Wallman. Special thanks go to David Wargo, who provided additional support for the TCI and Capital Cities chapters.

I'd also like to thank my father, Nick Thorndike, for his close readings and insights, and my wonderful children, Charlotte and Nicholas, for their patience with this project, for welcome distractions at critical junctures along the way, and for occasional wisdom beyond their years. I also benefitted from early research assistance from Elizabeth and Amory Thorndike.

I'd like to especially thank Charlie Munger, Warren Buffett's inimitable partner, for his early encouragement of this project and for his insightful comments, particularly on the Teledyne, Capital Cities, Washington Post, and General Dynamics chapters.

I'd also like to offer special thanks to Denise Ahern, my unflappable, omni-competent assistant, for her exceptional help and support (and patience) over these last almost nine years.

Thanks also to Charlotte MacDonald for all of her excellent support over the years.

My agent, David Miller, was a constant source of insight and perspective throughout the project.

My editors, Jeff Kehoe and Allison Peter, and their Harvard Business Review Press team did an excellent job, shepherding and guiding the manuscript and its inexperienced author through the stages of the publishing process.

Last, I'd like to thank Genie, my indispensable "in-house" editor (and wife), for her invaluable, tough-minded, provocative readings of the manuscript in its various stages of life and for her unfailing support over many years.

Any mistakes are, of course, all my own, but the wisdom and support of this group immeasurably improved the final product. Thank you, thank you.

# Appendix:
# The Buffett Test

Warren Buffett has proposed a simple test of capital allocation ability: has a CEO created at least a dollar of value for every dollar of retained earnings over the course of his tenure? Buffett's metric captures in a single number the collective wisdom and folly of decision-making over the course of an entire career. Sadly, it is a tougher test than it sounds and not surprisingly, these outsider CEOs passed with flying colors, as table A-1 demonstrates.

**TABLE A-1**

## Outsider CEOs and the Buffett test

| | Berkshire Hathaway | General Cinema/ Harcourt General* | Teledyne | Capital Cities/ABC | Washington Post | TCI** | Ralston Purina | General Dynamics |
|---|---|---|---|---|---|---|---|---|
| **Target period** | | | | | | | | |
| Start date | June 30, 1965 | January 31, 1966 | May 31, 1963 | September 30, 1966 | June 30, 1971 | May 31, 1973 | January 31, 1980 | December 31, 1990 |
| End date | September 30, 2010 | July 31, 2001 | June 30, 1990 | December 31, 1995 | December 31, 1993 | March 31, 1999 | December 31, 2001 | December 31, 2007 |
| **Buffet test years** | | | | | | | | |
| Start | 1965 | 1962 | 1966 | 1966 | 1971 | 1973 | 1981 | 1990 |
| End | 2007 | 2000 | 1989 | 1994 | 1993 | 1997 | 2000 | 2007 |
| Cumulative "Buffett ratio" | 2.3 times | 3.6 times | 2.0 times | 2.7 times | 1.9 times | n/a | 2.4 times | 3.5 times |

* The General Cinema data adjusts for extreme swings associated with the 1991 Harcourt General acquisition, which otherwise skews the data.

** Malone managed TCI to intentionally minimize reported earnings; therefore, this metric does not apply to him.

# Notes

*Preface*

1. Berkshire Hathaway annual reports, 1987.

2. Ibid.

3. Warren E. Buffett, "The Superinvestors of Graham and Doddville," *Hermes* Magazine, April 1984.


*Introduction*

1. Atul Gawande, "The Bell Curve," *The New Yorker,* December 6, 2004. See also Richard Pascale, Jerry Sternin, and Monique Sternin, *The Power of Positive Deviance: How Unlikely Innovators Solve the World's Toughest Problems* (Boston: Harvard Business Press, 2010).

2. Michael Lewis, *Moneyball: The Art of Winning an Unfair Game* (New York: W.W. Norton and Company, 2003).

3. Malcolm Gladwell, *Outliers: The Story of Success* (New York: Little, Brown and Co., 2008)

4. Robert J. Flaherty, "The Singular Henry Singleton," *Forbes,* July 9, 1979.


*Chapter 1*

1. Charles T. Munger memo, January 1, 1983.

2. Unless otherwise noted, all quotations from Tom Murphy come from a telephone interview on March 23, 2005, and an in-person interview on July 25, 2005.

3. "Tom Murphy's Pleasant Cash Problem," *Forbes,* October 1, 1976.

4. Author interview with Dan Burke, April 1, 2005.

5. Author interview with Gordon Crawford, April 20, 2005.

6. Author interview with Bob Zelnick, March 23, 2005.

7. Author interview with Dan Burke, April 1, 2005.

8. Author interview with Phil Beuth, April 28, 2005.

9. Author interview with Dan Burke, April 1, 2005.

10. "Tom Murphy's Pleasant Cash Problem."

11. Author interview with David Wargo, April 28, 2005.

12. Author interview with Gordon Crawford, April 20, 2005.

13. Author interview with Phil Meek, April 1, 2005.


*Chapter 2*

1. Author interview with Jack Hamilton, April 20, 2004.

2. Robert J. Flaherty, "The Sphinx Speaks," *Forbes,* February 20, 1978.

3. Author interview with Charles T. Munger, September 10, 2004.

4. Author interview with Arthur Rock, April 15, 2004.

5. Author interview with Charles T. Munger, September 10, 2004.

6. Ibid.

7. Author interview with Fayez Sarofim, March 2, 2004.

8. Author interview with William Rutledge, February 23, 2004.

9. James P. Roscow, "The Many Lives of Teledyne," *Financial World,* November 1, 1978.

10. Robert J. Flaherty, "The Singular Henry Singleton," *Forbes,* July 9, 1979.

11. Flaherty, "The Sphinx Speaks."

12. Author interview with Leon Cooperman, November 20, 2003.


*Chapter 3*

1. Author interview with William Anders, April 5, 2008.

2. Unless otherwise noted, all quotations from William Anders come from telephone interviews on April 15 and April 24, 2008.

3. Author interview with Ray Lewis, March 20, 2008.

4. Author interview with Peter Aseritis, March 7, 2008.

5. Author interview with James Mellor, March 12, 2008.

6. Author interview with Peter Aseritis, March 7, 2008.

7. Author interview with James Mellor, March 12, 2008.

8. Author interview with Nicholas Chabraja, April 2, 2008.

9. Author interview with Ray Lewis, March 20, 2008.

10. Author interview with Nicholas Chabraja, April 2, 2008.

11. Ibid.

12. Author interview with Ray Lewis, March 20, 2008.

13. Ibid.

## Chapter 4

1. Unless otherwise noted, all quotations from John Malone came from an in-person interview on April 30, 2007.

2. Author interview with J.C. Sparkman, April 30, 2007.

3. David Wargo TCI analyst report, 1981.

4. Author interview with Dennis Leibowitz, April 17, 2007.

5. Author interview with Rick Reiss, April 26, 2007.

6. Author interview with David Wargo, April 17, 2007.

7. Author interview with Rick Reiss, April 26, 2007.

8. David Wargo TCI analyst report, 1980.

9. David Wargo interview/analyst report.

10. Author interview with Dennis Leibowitz, April 17, 2007.

11. David Wargo TCI interview/analyst report, 1982.

12. Author interview with Dennis Leibowitz, April 17, 2007.

13. David Wargo TCI analyst reports, 1981, 1982.

14. Ibid.

15. Author interview with David Wargo, April 17, 2007.

## Chapter 5

1. Author interview with Alan Spoon, April 2, 2009.

2. Author interview with Tom Might, April 30, 2009.

3. Unless otherwise noted, all quotations from Donald Graham came from an in-person interview in his office on April 3, 2009.

4. Author interview with George Gillespie, April 8, 2009.

5. Author interview with Ross Glotzbach, March 30, 2009.

6. Author interview with George Gillespie, April 8, 2009.

7. Author interview with Alan Spoon, April 2, 2009.

8. Author interview with Dick Simmons, April 22, 2009.

9. Author interview with Ben Bradlee in his office, April 3, 2009.

## Chapter 6

1. Author interview with Michael Mauboussin, February 25, 2009.
2. Ibid.
3. Author interview with Pat Mulcahy, April 23, 2009.
4. Unless otherwise noted, all quotations from William Stiritz came from numerous telephone interviews in April, May, and June, 2009.
5. Author interview with Pat Mulcahy, April 23, 2009.
6. Ibid.
7. Author interview with Michael Mauboussin, February 24, 2009.
8. Author interview with John McMillin, April 2, 2009.
9. Author interview with John Bierbusse, February 24, 2009.

## Chapter 7

1. Author interview with Bob Beck, February 26, 2008.
2. Author interview with Woody Ives, December 15, 2007.
3. Author interview with Caesar Sweitzer, April 22, 2008.
4. Ibid.
5. Author interview with Woody Ives, December 15, 2007.
6. Author interview with Bob Beck, March 26, 2008.
7. Author interview with David Wargo, April 22, 2008.
8. Unless otherwise noted, all quotations from Dick Smith are from an in-person interview on April 23, 2009, at his office in Chestnut Hill, MA.
9. Author interview with Woody Ives, December 15, 2007.
10. Ibid.
11. Author interview with Woody Ives, December 15, 2007.

## Chapter 8

1. Author interview with Charles T. Munger, February 24, 2006.
2. Berkshire Hathaway annual reports, 1977–2011.
3. Ibid.
4. Unless otherwise noted, all quotations came from interviews with Warren E. Buffett, July 24, 2006.
5. Author interview with Charles T. Munger, February 24, 2006.
6. Berkshire Hathaway annual reports, 1977–2011.
7. "The World's Top Investing Stars," *Money Week,* July 6, 2006.
8. Berkshire Hathaway annual reports, 1977–2011.

9. Author interview with David Sokol, April 15, 2006.

10. Berkshire Hathaway annual reports, Owner's Manual.

11. Author interview with Tom Murphy, March 9, 2006.

12. Author interview with Charles T. Munger, February 24, 2006.

13. Berkshire Hathaway annual reports, 1977–2011.

14. Berkshire Hathaway annual reports, 1977–2011.


*Chapter 9*

1. Daniel Kahneman, *Thinking, Fast and Slow* (New York: Farrar, Straus and Giroux, 2011).

2. Author interview with George Roberts, April 8, 2004.

3. Author interview with Charles T. Munger, September 10, 2004.

4. Author interview with Pat Mulcahy, April 23, 2009.

5. Andrew Barry, "What a Gusher," *Barron's,* November 16, 2009.

6. Michiyo Nakamoto and David Wighton, "Citigroup Chief Stays Bullish on Buy-outs," *Financial Times,* July 9, 2007.


*Epilogue*

1. Atul Gawande, *The Checklist Manifesto: How to Get Things Right* (New York: Metropolitan Books, 2010).

# Further Reading

Auletta, Ken. *The Highwaymen: Warriors of the Information Super Highway.* New York: Harcourt, Brace and Company, 1997.

Auletta, Ken. *Three Blind Mice: How the TV Networks Lost Their Way.* New York: Random House, 1991.

Bernstein, Peter L. *Against the Gods: The Remarkable Story of Risk.* New York: John Wiley and Sons, 1996.

Biggs, Barton. *Hedge hogging.* Hoboken, NJ: John Wiley and Sons, 2006.

The Buffett Partnership. Collection of Reports to Investors, 1958–1969.

Byrne, John A. *The Whiz Kids: The Founding Fathers of American Business and the Legacy They Left Us.* New York: Currency/Doubleday, 1993.

Conant, Jennet. *Tuxedo Park: A Wall Street Tycoon and the Secret Palace of Science That Changed the Course of World War II.* New York: Simon & Schuster, 2002.

Cunningham, Lawrence. *The Essays of Warren Buffett: Lessons for Corporate America.* Durham, NC: Carolina Academic Press, 1997.

Drucker, Peter F. *Adventures of a Bystander.* New York: Harper and Row, 1978.

Ellis, Charles D., ed. (with James R. Vertin). *Classics: An Investor's Anthology.* Homewood, IL: Dow Jones-Irwin, 1989.

Gladwell, Malcom. *Outliers: The Story of Success.* New York: Little, Brown, and Company, 2008.

Gleick, James. *The Information: A History, a Theory, a Flood.* New York: Vintage Books, 2011.

Graham, Katharine. *Personal History.* New York: A.A. Knopf, 1997.

Hagstrom, R.G. *The Warren Buffett Portfolio.* New York: John Wiley and Sons, 1999.

Halberstam, David. *The Best and the Brightest.* New York: Random House, 1972.

Kahneman, Daniel. *Thinking, Fast and Slow.* New York: Farrar, Straus, and Giroux, 2011.

Kaufman, Peter D. *Poor Charlie's Almanack: The Wit and Wisdom of Charles T. Munger.* Los Angeles: PCA Publications, 2005.

Kuhn, Thomas S. *The Structure of Scientific Revolutions.* Chicago: University of Chicago Press, 1996.

Lawrence, Mary Wells. *A Big Life (in Advertising).* New York: Simon & Schuster, 2002.

Lowe, Janet. *Damn Right! Behind the Scenes with Berkshire Hathaway Billionaire Charlie Munger.* New York: John Wiley and Sons, 2000.

Lowenstein, Roger. *Buffett: The Making of an American Capitalist.* New York: Random House, 1995.

Mauboussin, Michael. *More Than You Know: Finding Financial Wisdom in Unconventional Places.* New York: Columbia University Press, 2006.

Poundstone, William. *Fortune's Formula: The Untold Story of the Scientific Betting System That Beat the Casinos and Wall Street.* New York: Hill and Wang, 2005.

Press, Eyal. *Beautiful Souls: Saying No, Breaking Ranks, and Heeding the Voice of Conscience in Dark Times.* New York: Farrar, Straus, and Giroux, 2012.

Preston, Richard. *American Steel.* New York: Avon Books, 1992.

Pruitt, Bettye H. *The Making of Harcourt General: A History of Growth Through Diversification 1922–1992.* Boston: Harvard Business School Press, 1994.

Roberts, John. *The Modern Firm: Organizational Design for Performance and Growth.* New York: Oxford University Press, 2004.

Robichaux, Mark. *Cable Cowboy: John Malone and the Rise of the Modern Cable Business.* Hoboken, NJ: John Wiley and Sons, 2002.

Skildelsky, Robert. *John Maynard Keynes, Volume 2: The Economist as Savior, 1920–1937.* New York: Penguin Books, 1995.

Swensen, David F. *Unconventional Success: A Fundamental Approach to Personal Investment.* New York: Free Press, 2005.

Tedlow, Richard S. *Giants of Enterprise: Seven Business Innovators and the Empires They Built.* New York: Harper Business, 2001.

Train, John. *The Money Masters.* New York: Harper and Row, 1980.

# Index

# About the Author

**Will Thorndike** is a graduate of Harvard College and the Stanford Graduate School of Business. He is the founder and managing director of Housatonic Partners, an investment firm with offices in Boston and San Francisco. Prior to that he worked with T. Rowe Price Associates, where he did early investment research in the field of business services, and Walker Publishing, where he later served on the board of directors.

Will has lectured at the Harvard and Stanford Business Schools, as well as at INSEAD and the London Business School. He is currently a director at Alta Colleges; Continental Fire & Safety Services; Carillon Assisted Living; LeMaitre Vascular; Liberty Towers; Oasis Group Ltd.; QMC International; and White Flower Farm. He is a trustee of the Stanford Business School Trust and College of the Atlantic and a member of the board of overseers at WGBH. Will is also a founding partner at FARM, a social impact investing collaborative. He lives outside of Boston with his wife and two children.